BOXES

BOXES

Lifting the Lid on an American Life

Donnan Beeson Runkel

To order additional copies of this book, contact:
Xlibris Corporation
1-888-795-4274
www.Xlibris.com
Orders@Xlibris.com
76157

Contents

Dedicated to dear, beloved David Runkel,
who long ago gave me a monogrammed, empty red leather book
and urged me to write in it.
Without his encouragement and loving support, that book
and this one, would still be empty.

Why Boxes?

For many years, my economic and professional value was deposited on a resumé, all of me reduced to two pages of twelve-point type. But the resumé never told anyone what events defined my life or with which elixir it was laced. It had no space for the hollowness of my teen years or the seeds of my addiction to activism. In its many iterations, it said nothing about my career as a parent, or my treatment for depression. It concealed the fact that members of my family struggled with alcohol and my mother purposely aborted the child before me. It said nothing of the impact my resident Victorian grandmother had upon me. While it noted my various jobs at Peace Corps spanning more than eight years, it didn't have "Triumph!" written in the margins.

One day as I passed by the dresser in my bedroom, I paused to take in the collection of decorative boxes crowded together on top. "There's my life right there," I said out loud. My story in tin and sterling silver, in porcelain and wood, painted and plain, small and large, each one given to me by someone who in some way made me who I am. While they may function as containers for my jewelry, more importantly they are placeholders for the people, the times and the places of my life. The relationships that formed me, the tragedies that befell me, the unexpected joy that overcame me—they're all held there inside those boxes on top of the lacy dresser scarf covering the big mahogany dresser that used to hold Granny's linens.

Writing the stories held in these boxes has helped to organize my life in my mind, to make some sense of how my life has turned out. What did I learn? Could I have done it better? What did I give—and what did I receive? In the process of opening these boxes and the relationships they contained, I've found some answers. I discovered things I hadn't expected. Family patterns came clear. Encumbrances dissipated and fell away. I discovered myself as a hybrid full of rich seeds.

Writing *Boxes* became an unexpected rite of passage to a new level of understanding. I found the authenticity I'd spent a great deal of my life seeking.

Different from my resumé, with its emphasis on the work I did, *Boxes* reveals the work I became.

Donnan Beeson Runkel
Ashland, Oregon
June 2010

CHAPTER ONE

Paragon of Perfection

"All right," I screeched, "go ahead and talk about Daddy Mac in front of me. I'm sorry, I'm sorry I killed him. I didn't mean to. Don't torture me anymore about this." Across the table Mother and Granny both muttered that I was being ridiculous.

"Settle down there, Donnan, we're having a perfectly nice dinner," Granny said.

My mother, always in lock-step with her mother, chimed in. "Stop it right now, before you have to leave the table." I "stopped it right now" and left at my own behest, stomping up the stairs, sobbing. The elephant on the table inside me propelled me to my dark bedroom, hysterical. I was twelve years old and killing my grandfather had been hidden in me for so long, I could hardly believe it was finally out. It was the flaw no one had seen before this evening. All those years when I had to wear my sister's hand-me-downs, I'd wondered if it was because child criminals like me didn't deserve new dresses like she did.

Whenever my grandmother talked about Daddy Mac or asked if I remembered this time or that, I'd freeze, afraid that she would accuse me outright of ruining her life, cutting short the time she'd had with the man she loved. It was me who had forced her into widowhood and life with our family in place of her wonderful house in Waynesburg, Pennsylvania, that had always smelled of lavender and something freshly baked.

My involvement in Daddy Mac's death all started one day when my mother and Granny had gone shopping, leaving me with a grandfather I didn't know had terminal cancer. I was about five. A game developed in which I would pull books off the shelf, toss them at him, and he would catch them.

Mother and Granny were horrified at the scene they returned to—an exhausted grandfather and his granddaughter curled up reading together, books scattered everywhere. I was sent to bed without dinner. I don't know how long afterward it was, but the next thing I knew, my grandfather was dead. No autopsy was necessary for me. I knew I'd cut him down with all those books.

I'd successfully avoided the topic for years, until that period of adolescence when stomping away from the dinner table would be as inevitable as rain in April.

My sobbing subsided. I covered my hot face with the cool side of my beloved down pillow. The door to my room opened and in came my father. I peeked out from under the pillow, my eyes squinting tightly as light penetrated my darkness.

"Your grandfather had cancer. That's what he died of," Daddy said right out, putting his hand on my hunched shoulder. I was curled up in a ball, trying to control a bad case of post-hysteria hiccups. "I don't know where you ever got the idea that you were responsible, but you weren't, Dee. Now come on down and finish your dinner. You always love Spanish rice." He left, leaving the door open. That was the last time the subject was ever mentioned.

When we moved to suburban Philadelphia just after Daddy Mac's death, Granny came with us. While other households I knew also contained three generations, it always seemed to me that none was as oddly sorted as ours. My mother and father's room was in the back of the house. Mine was next to theirs, and then came my older brother Bill's. In the master bedroom suite, with its own bath, lived Granny and my sister Nettie, her namesake. They slept in a double bed, and the bond they shared was not what the rest of us had with our grandmother. I don't know how or why this arrangement ever came about, but in my mind the decision-making process might have begun, and ended, with a conversation something like this:

"Well, dear, I plan to share a room with Netts when I come to live with you," Granny says.

"But Mother, she and Donnan can share a room just as well. That's the way it should be, don't you think?"

"No, Nettie and I will be together. That's how it will be."

That was Granny, and while she did indulge all of us, Nettie was *special*. Granny dressed us all, expensively and elegantly, but each season meant a completely new wardrobe for Nettie. My clothing needs were dictated more by what I "needed." She paid for some lessons for all of us, but Nettie got the most—dancing classes, art classes, ice skating, tennis and riding lessons.

Granny held sway in our house. At the dinner table, our behavior was monitored carefully by this very small round woman with sky blue eyes. Should we say something she considered untoward, we were subjected to a clawing hand on our thigh if we were next to her, or a scowl and slight shake of the head if we were across the table.

Granny was the authority on nearly everything. What we should wear. With whom we should be friends. What we should read at what age. How to play bridge. What was *good* music. (Stravinsky was much too modern.) What birds came to the feeder outside her window. How to bake. What made a "good drink," and what you should drink when. (Martinis are murderous; no gin until after Memorial Day.) How to score tennis. What art should be appreciated most.

At Christmas, we got to be her wrapping and baking assistant. *Always make your folds sharp on your wrapping paper and your bows big. When storing cookies, always put wax paper between each layer in every tin, and hide an extra tin of pecan puffs so your father won't eat all of them.* After school, I'd sit in her room laden with blue and white chintz and learn the names of the birds while marking my favorite things in the Christmas catalogues with a "D."

Because my father traveled regularly for business, and my mother was one of the few in those days who worked outside the home, Granny played an indispensable role in our household. As did her checkbook—which made major contributions to the wellbeing of our family. My parents had both grown up with all the advantages Granny could now ensure our generation.

Even though she was only in her fifties when she came to live with us, she seemed older, probably because she wore a steel gray wig. Each week a package from The American Transformation Company in New York would arrive with a clean version of Granny's hair. Her coif had waves along each side that folded neatly into a bun in the back. At night it rested on a muslin head on her dresser and she went to bed bald, the sight of which always scared me a little and made me wonder what it was like for Nettie to sleep with a pink-headed person.

The great Influenza Outbreak of 1919 had snatched away every hair on Granny's head. I'm afraid finding that out didn't exactly awaken my compassion for this calamity in her life. That hairless head became one of my featured tourist attractions for friends spending the night. When I was sure she was asleep, I'd offer peeks into her room, taking care not to let the doorknob squeak too loudly.

My friends loved to come to our house, and despite Granny's hair situation, each of them had her own enduring relationship with her. If some of us didn't have dates to a school dance, Granny would become our host. She'd make fresh cinnamon rolls and coach us on what steps to take to ensure we got dates to the next prom. (And she didn't say a word if we ate a whole half gallon of vanilla fudge ice cream after the cinnamon buns.) She thought we should read *Sports Illustrated*, so we could discuss sports with the boys. (She was a charter subscriber.) We should learn to play bridge. She taught us. We should know where all the most notable colleges are. She drilled us. We should have opinions about current events. She thought we should read the *Atlantic* and the Sunday *New York Times*.

Being relieved of the burden of killing my grandfather had opened a new era in my relationship with Granny, and we grew quite close. We spent many afternoons, weekends and evenings together when the rest of the family was out socializing. I knew I'd never *be* Nettie, but I aspired to learning everything Granny thought I ought to so that, like Nettie, *I* would one day have dates that would eventually land me in a marriage.

"Come here, pet, sit down," she'd say. I'd sit on the floor beside the armchair where she always sat and Granny would caress my head, telling me how luminous and silky my dark brown hair was. I'd lean back, awash in nurture for just a moment before the next piece of advice came crashing down. "When you laugh loud, darling, boys don't like it at all."

One night I told her I thought I'd never fit in with the people who had dates. All this effort was useless. Impatient, she said, "You come from a very fine family and have a lot to be proud about."

"But Granny, being from a fine old family is not getting me dates or helping me swim faster in races or be better on the hockey field. I'm just plain ugly, especially with all these braces on my teeth. It's just not ever going to work for me, no matter how hard I try." My eyes filled up with tears. "You tell me if I know things, boys will ask me to dances. It's just not true."

"You haven't *really* tried yet, dearie, have you?" she said.

In Granny's world, lurking behind every corner was the likelihood I wouldn't do the right thing. One summer toward the end of high school, I finally had a boy friend. I was away at camp as a counselor-in-training. No matter how many letters I sent him, he never wrote back, except once. I'd complained about this in a letter home. Granny wrote back in her classic, rounded handwriting:

Darling, don't feel too bad if Peter doesn't write—not many boys his age are good correspondents, and it doesn't necessarily mean he doesn't still like you. I only hope he didn't hear that you made fun of his letter and read it to all the girls. Boys hate that!

In return for Granny's tutelage at home, we kept her plied with bourbon and water.

"Donnan, this drink looks awfully weak. You must not have given it enough of the brown stuff," she would say with a pout.

"Maybe I just put too much water in, Gran."

"We can fix *that*, can't we," she'd say, handing the glass back, her lips firmly pressed together.

⌘

When I got ready to leave for college, my wardrobe was assembled by Granny, the key ingredient being to attract the "right" men, which seemed to be the reason why I was going to college. A basic black dress from Peck & Peck. A red Bardley suit from Best & Co. A kilt made in Scotland. A camel's hair coat. Shetland sweaters with my monogram on them. Granny was not pleased that I ended up going to Penn State, or as she called it, a "land-grant" university, and not a women's college. Granny herself had gone to Emma Willard, a "finishing school" in Troy, New York, where she must have learned that clothes and looks were essential to success in life. While Granny thought it was a good thing I'd be majoring in English, because reading was important, no one seemed interested in the fact that I wanted to write, or that the famous novelist John Barth was my advisor.

Once I got to my land-grant university, I didn't find much use for all Granny's stratagems, aphorisms or wardrobe advice. Practically no one knew how to play bridge. No one really cared where the "good" colleges were, and there were precious few occasions where I needed to wear a good wool suit or know which spoon or fork to use first and last. Persistent in her efforts on my behalf, Granny gave me a trip to College Week in Bermuda and the necessary fine wardrobe to go with it. As the Pan Am flight from Idlewild Airport took off, I still believed Granny's preparations would create the magic that would at last make me the belle of the ball. Amidst the beauty of Bermuda, the human being she had primed to be interesting and irresistible would emerge

Alas, the only luster of the whole experience was the tan that resulted from a terrible sunburn. Not one young man's head was turned when I appeared for dinner in my black linen dress. Not one of the many college boys there flocked to my side to discuss the latest basketball news. Those I did meet didn't seem to notice what I wore or that I knew where Oberlin College was or that Cleveland's Rocky Colavito was only the third player in history to hit four consecutive home runs.

Not long after I got back from Bermuda, my friend Peggy burst into my dorm room. She'd just returned from Wayne, Pennsylvania, where we'd grown up together.

"Granny looks like hell, but I think she's going to pull through. She sent you her love," she reported.

"What? I didn't even know she was sick. What are you talking about? Why didn't my parents call me?" I started to cry.

"Really, Donnan, my mother said it's just her heart again. Dr. Hanes was there when I went by."

I brushed past her and ran to the pay phone to make a collect call home. I'd never even considered a life without Granny.

"Mother, Peggy says Granny's really sick." I was shaking. "What's going on?" I sputtered, before beginning to cry again.

"Oh, Dee, don't worry. We've taken her to the hospital, and she'll be fine. Her feet were just a little swollen," my mother said matter-of-factly.

"Do you think I should come home? Peggy says she looks awful."

"Peggy is not a doctor, Donnan. Now you just better get back to your studies," my mother said. "We'll let you know if things change. Let's not run up the long distance phone bill. You be good."

The next day, my father called to say that Granny had died. I was devastated. I didn't know what I would do without her. She was the one who always wanted to know what I was reading *and* even what I was writing. She always plied me with local news about things she knew I cared about.

A month later I returned home for my first visit since her death. I went directly to her room, where for the first time I felt like an intruder. It was the same as when I'd last seen it, but devoid of the lavender scent I'd treasured. My mother had said it would be all right if I took a small memento. The crystal jar with cotton balls in it caught my eye. Round and beautiful like Granny, I thought. Brilliant little squares laced with lines of light reflected outside and in. The lid fit exactly. It made me think of how she wanted each of us to be cut so fine and perfect.

Every time I lift that delicate lid, I can almost hear the voice of its original owner dispensing her quintessential advice: *Donnan, darling. It's important to do the right thing. And if you're worried that you won't, just sit like a bunny and act like you was one.*

I tried for so many years to sit like that damned bunny, until I finally realized that it was a failed strategy. I wasn't happy. I wasn't fulfilled in ways I wanted to be.

Now, as I lift the crystal lid, that little paragon of perfection, I can speak to her from a different life: Granny, so much of how I live is what you wanted for me. I read *The New York Times* and the *New Yorker* regularly. I'm well-dressed and unfailingly polite. I'm married to a handsome, intelligent and successful man. Our guests at the B&B enjoy your beautiful furniture, silver and recipes. But what they enjoy the most is that we do the right thing *our* way, every day.

CHAPTER TWO

Normal

"Mom, that man fondled my breasts when I was sound asleep next to David down at the shore. And you and Daddy kept on being friends with him until you discovered he *cheated at bridge.*" Across the phone lines, my voice was sizzling at her latest news. "That's incredible. I can't believe it. Is that what you're telling me?"

"Donnan, you're blowing this out of proportion, really. Your father and I just don't want to play bridge with him now that we know he cheats. What he did or didn't do to you at the shore doesn't enter into it."

I got off the phone feeling angry and abandoned.

My mother just wasn't a normal mother—at least what I thought was normal. I always wanted her to wear a matching bathing cap and suit like so many of the others did. Those mothers had sleek Rose Marie Reid bathing suits, caps that covered hairdresser hair-do's, and good tans. My mother wore cotton prints, no cap, did her own hair with help from Clairol and was lily white because she worked fulltime. When I compared her to my friends' mothers in Wayne, Pennsylvania, she simply didn't fit the model. *Did that mean I didn't fit the model either?*

Since my mother failed to fall into the "typical" categories, I was never totally certain what to call her. Over the years I tried everything from Mummy to Mother to Lucy to Mum to Muzzy to Mimi and Mom. I think I may have been trying to invent a normal mother for myself by dint of name. Maybe if I called her Mummy, she'd become the perfect mother and focus on what charms should be on my gold charm bracelet. Maybe if I called her Mother she would come to my swim meets and make sure I had a dry towel after every race like Alice Marks's mother did. Maybe if I called her Muzzy, she would be a little like Auntie Mame. My friend Penny Weller called her mother by her first name, and they seemed to be actual friends. So for a while I tried calling her Lucy, but we didn't seem to get any friendlier. I think she wasn't sure about who she was to me either. Letters I received at camp each summer were variably signed, "Devotedly, Mother," or "Luce," or "Mama."

She was also the only mother I knew who worked at what was considered a *real* job. She was the Quartermaster at Valley Forge Military Academy, and she was proud of it. One night, however, during dessert at the St. David's Golf Club, her career came to an abrupt end. Frank Rackley, the president of my father's steel company, declared, "Lucy, we just can't have our executives' wives working. You'd better let Valley Forge know as soon as possible that you're resigning."

I remember my mother mounting a meek protest.

"But Frank, I *like* working. And we'll have Bill, Jr.'s college tuition to pay . . . "

"Lucy, it just doesn't look good. We need both you and Bill to be full-time ambassadors for Jessop Steel."

When Frank Rackley came to town, it was always momentous, but this was huge. My mother quitting her job? I wasn't sure it would really happen. They'd all had a lot to drink, and at twelve years old, I clearly knew what that could mean—lots of things got said you really couldn't count on. Alcohol regularly brought a cloud of unpredictability upon our house, but when Mr. Rackley was around, even more than usual got consumed. I hadn't looked forward to his visit, but this particular turn of events held promise. I went to bed wondering—maybe Mimi/ Mom/Mother would stop working and we could be a normal family.

The day right after Mr. Rackley's demand, Mother's resignation did go in. General Baker, the head of Valley Forge, called my father to protest, but to no avail. After that, whenever Mother and Daddy got into one of their regular fights, she would always threaten to go back to work.

"You just watch, Bill Beeson. I'll get a job no matter *what* you and Frank Rackley say." I'd hear her raised voice from behind their closed bedroom door. "I've still got the General's recommendation. *He* knows what I can do."

The normal mother I'd yearned for never materialized. Even though she wasn't working, she still didn't come to my swim meets, help organize events at school or take me shopping for clothes. She didn't even have a driver's license.

Knowing that my mother had loved working herself, years later when I had my own family, I felt certain she'd be supportive when I decided to return to work. The children were a little younger than I had been when she started a job, but I hoped this common path we shared might bring us closer or make us more compatible. Instead, she was horrified. And I was horrified that she was horrified.

"David has a perfectly good job, it's just ridiculous for you to be off working," she said when I told her I'd been hired as a writer for a PR agency a few days a week.

"I'm doing it to preserve my sanity, and besides, it's only part-time. Also, the furniture needs to be reupholstered, we don't have one rug in the house, and there are all kinds of other things we could afford if I worked. Besides, *you* worked. Why are you upset that I am?"

"When I first got the job, your father was out of work. I *had* to. It wasn't for my sanity. I was doing it so we'd have money to eat."

"Yes, but even after Daddy got a job you kept on working until Frank Rackley . . . "

"You're being ridiculous, Donnan. That was a long time ago."

A year later I learned that I had to have two major surgeries in a row. The doctor said I'd have to be on the second floor of our Baltimore townhouse for at least a week after a long hospital stay. Hope sprang anew that I would have a mother who would lovingly help me out during my convalescence. In fact, I *yearned* to know I could be taken care of by my mother. I felt sure she'd come when she heard how much I'd need her. She was newly widowed and a short train ride away in Philadelphia, without much but bridge club, Benson & Hedges cigarettes and bourbon to occupy herself. Besides, she'd always talked about how Granny came to help when she'd had surgery and felt overwhelmed. Anticipating a new phase in our relationship, I called her on the phone to ask.

"Are you sure you need to have this surgery, or are you just being a hypochondriac again?" she asked.

"Mom, I'm not making this up," I countered. "He's a well-known surgeon and the people at Johns Hopkins agree it's the only choice left at this point."

"I have to check my calendar and call you back," she said. End of conversation. *Was it me or was it her?*

A day later she called back. "I just can't do it, Donnan, there's too much going on up here. Bloodmobile day is next Tuesday, the regular bridge club is here Wednesday, the Sandwich bridge is here on Friday, and my symphony tickets are Thursday night." I got off the phone bitterly disappointed and began calling our friends. They all pitched in and quickly organized a schedule of who would help which day.

Lee Hoffman was eighty years old and the first to arrive. Besides lavishing me with love and affection, he established a routine for all the other helpers as well. He'd pick Marshall up at kindergarten, feed him lunch, bring me a glass of what he said was medicinal sherry, put both children down for naps and then fix my lunch. I was in a constant state of advanced gratitude *and* guilt that other people were doing all these things for me that my mother should have been doing. It was downright embarrassing, and I felt sure they all thought less of me for having a slacker for a mother.

One day Lee stopped me before my usual rant about my negligent mother got underway. "Deedie, wait a minute. Just this morning, Charlotte and I were talking about your mom. We want to have a dinner party for her when she is able to come."

"A dinner party? For my mother? How wonderful that you want to do that, but . . . . *why?*

"That's easy," he said. "We want to get to know whoever your mother is. Knowing you, she must be a very interesting, smart person."

I was stunned. What Lee said virtually turned me around. Even if I couldn't produce an on-site mother, he regarded me as an interesting, smart person. And my mother couldn't be all that bad if she'd produced a daughter like me. In one swift moment, I was relieved of all the guilt I felt for not being the daughter my mother seemed to want and not being the friend I figured Lee and his wife wanted. At the same time my mother was released from blame for not fulfilling my expectations of her as my mother. For the first time, I could see my mother more as a person than as someone capable on a daily basis of disappointing me.

The truth is my mother *was* a very smart and interesting person. Like her mother before her, she could quote poetry written in three different centuries, knew French and Latin better than most, was excellent at math. The table next to her big chair in the living room always had a stack of books on top of it as well as on its lower shelf. When it was time to choose which Book-of-the-Month Club book to order, she knew what she wanted because she read the *New York Times Book Review* cover to cover every week. The fact that her presence was more an absence in my childhood, and that I never really felt close to her, didn't deny her place in the world as a human being.

She was also a good musician, and music was always a part of our household. Many nights after dinner my mother would play from the big thick green book of American folksongs, and we would all sing. Participation was not optional, so whenever I invited someone for a sleepover, I would warn them (at the last minute so they wouldn't back out) that there would probably be singing after dinner.

These sing-a-longs were part joy and part torture for me. While I had a good soprano voice, I had a special knack for going off pitch or missing a note, which Mother would deal with by telling me to sit down as she played merrily on with my brother singing baritone and my sister alto.

"Donnan, don't you see it's a "G" not an "F?" she'd ask, at the end of the song, alternately pounding on the two keys.

She heard every note I sang, but rarely what was on my mind. A good example of this was the famous weekend when

David and I were at the beach with my parents and some of their friends, and I awoke to find my breast being fondled by one of the men. With my husband sleeping right next to me! After breakfast, I took my parents aside, told them what had happened and announced we were returning home unless that reprehensible man was told he was no longer welcome. My mother said I shouldn't make such a big deal of it.

"Donnan, don't let yourself get so upset by this. It really isn't worth the fuss. For heaven's sake, just enjoy being here at the shore. We don't even know him very well, so it would be awkward for your father to talk to him anyway."

"But, mother, he *felt* me. That's just plain creepy, and he's a total creep, and I can't believe you and Daddy are ever going to speak to him again," I shot back. David and I left after breakfast. It was not the first nor the last time that alcohol and their drinking friends trumped my parents' regard for my wellbeing.

❦

The ravages of alcohol and emphysema caught up with my mother when she was in her early sixties. All of our efforts to convince her to change her lifestyle had been for naught. When she was told to cut down on cigarettes, she switched from Pall Malls to Lucky Strikes, because they were shorter. When I suggested I was uncomfortable continuing to buy her bourbon, she got the cab company to deliver it. She eventually decided bowling was too hard on her joints and quit her only form of exercise. The time between hospitalizations grew shorter and shorter.

When David and I bought our house in the Overbrook section of Philadelphia, one of its big selling points had been the "mother-in-law apartment." I'd told the realtor we'd be using it for a rental, since my mother would never consider moving in with *me*. But when we later offered it to her, she reluctantly accepted. We were delighted because it meant no longer traversing the fifty-three traffic lights between our two houses to check on her. Most importantly, she would be an adult presence when our kids got home from school. It was a relief from the babysitter anxiety I'd suffered nearly every day of my working years. I could tell the children Mimi would be there just like Granny, her mother, had been for me. I left out the part about Granny's cinnamon buns fresh from the oven, knowing there wasn't a chance Mimi would ever muster the energy to do that.

We helped pack up the apartment she'd lived in since my father's death nine years earlier. She was ready to "pitch things," as she put it.

"No need to pack that, dear. Just take it to Goodwill," she'd say each time I'd hesitate. How could I just send off touchstones from my childhood?

"Let's just take everything, Mother," I finally suggested. "There's plenty of room in your new apartment." As I gathered things up from the library table in the living room, I came upon the Florentine gilt box used for holding safety pins. I'd always loved it for its elegance and the beautiful bouquet hand-painted on its top.

"This has always been a favorite of mine." I said.

"Velma Zeigler brought me that years ago when she and Ed first went to Italy. I've always loved it too, but I don't know if it's because of the box or that I love who gave it to me. I miss Velma. But if you want it, dear, take it. It's pretty faded now, and I certainly don't need all those safety pins."

"Are you sure? Thanks. I'll have it to remember three things then—you, Velma and your friendship. Isn't that cool?" I asked.

"If you must, Donnan," she replied, wrapping it up in newspaper.

Each morning before I left for work, I'd go up to Mother's apartment to bring her breakfast and leave something for lunch. I'd discovered that if I didn't, she would just have a drink for lunch. One day when I'd called at noon to check what she was having, "Ice cubes" was the answer.

In return for my meal service, I typically got a running critique of what I was wearing and what I needed to be concerned about with the children. My skirt was too short, too long or not the right shade for the jacket. Had I checked with the orthodontist about Lucy's mouth yet, and I'd better be sure Marsh wrote his thank-you notes.

But for Marshall, Lucy and their friends, Mimi was a fountain of facts and fun. I'd get home to find the dining table in her apartment ringed with kids. If homework was done, they'd be playing Yahtzee. Julie Jones would be practicing her French. (Her grandmother, who *was* French, lived right behind us, but Julie thought it was more fun at our house.) Thoroughly enjoying being the life of the party, Mimi would be at the head of the table, cocktail in hand. Like Granny before her, she had long since trained one of her grandchildren in how to fix her "brown" drinks of bourbon and water once the clock struck five.

"Wow," I said one afternoon when I got home. "You all look really happy. Are you happy, Mimi?"

"It's your turn to roll the dice, Marshall," she responded, not even looking up at me.

Mimi was still in bed that morning when I took her coffee, toast and the newspaper. We chatted awhile. When I got up to go, I gave her a kiss on her forehead.

"You look awfully pretty today, darling," she said.

I was incredulous. "Really?"

Enveloped by a rare dose of mother love, I grabbed my briefcase and ran down the three flights of stairs, out the door and down the street in a dash to catch the 8:09 train. All day, I felt a special little lift in my spirits. I even checked the mirror in the Ladies Room to see if *I* thought I looked "awfully pretty."

When I got home that afternoon, the kids were all downstairs in our part of the house. "Why aren't you with Mimi like you're supposed to be," I asked, ready to remonstrate for breaking the rules.

"She's still napping," Lucy responded, returning to her book.

My heart racing, I ran upstairs to check. I found Mimi flung across the bed sideways.

For her memorial service, I wore the clothes Mother said I looked pretty in, and I had the soloist sing "Free at Last"—for both of us.

CHAPTER THREE

Legacy

It had been raining for several days when the flooding began. Whole sections of our end of town were going under water as Gulph Creek overran its banks. My father was an elected township commissioner, and constituents had begun calling to say their foundations were threatened. As always with constituent calls, it was the dinner hour.

Returning to the table, Daddy announced, "I'm going to have to borrow the neighbors' little boat and get down there to see the damage. They say the water is swirling up around their porches."

"Oh for Pete's sake, Bill, why do you have to ruin our dinner *again*?" my mother wanted to know.

"Luce, these people are desperate. I need to see what's going on and if there's anything we can do. C'mon, Dee, you can come with me." He pushed his six-foot, five-inch frame away from the table, unfolding upward. "We're going to have to pull that little trailer with the boat on it down to where the water begins. The Drapers are away, and I'm sure they won't mind our using it for this."

My mother recognized that her influence had been trumped by rising waters. "Get your slicker, Donnan. It's going to be wet and horrible," she said.

I was twelve years old and delighted to be chosen. But then again, there wasn't much choice. My mother was certainly not going to go. My big sister Nettie had no interest in political adventures with our father. I think she and my brother Bill thought Daddy's political activities were sort of embarrassing. But I liked it when our house filled up with people from nearby neighborhoods for meetings. Many of them had lots less than we did, and I liked it that Daddy seemed able to help them. It meant he was important, and that made me feel a little important too.

Daddy was my champion in the family. He drove me to swim practice all over three counties and came to meets when he could. He took my trophies and ribbons to the office to show off. And when he knew I was unhappy about not getting to go to camp for the summer, due to a shortage of funds, he sent me on my first solo plane trip to Washington, DC. He gave me important things to do. I loved going to political rallies with him, doorbell ringing, and didn't even mind looking up phone numbers from street lists so we could do telephone canvassing. This flood assignment was clearly a benefit of being a commissioner's daughter.

Daddy got into his big rubber coat and the green hip boots in which he'd campaigned for commissioner. He was the first ever to run a campaign wearing boots, to represent his call for our streams to be cleaned up. Eager to fill my role, I put on a sweat shirt and jeans and my red rubber boots with a zipper up the inside. My yellow slicker and sou'wester hat completed my storm ensemble.

We pulled the boat on its triangular trailer out of the Drapers' driveway and down the middle of Oak Lane. Even with Daddy doing most of the pulling, the weight of the trailer was making an imprint in my wet hands and stretching my arms until they felt a few inches longer. It was drizzling and still very dark.

In a couple of long blocks, we were wading in water, which soon went over the tops of my boots. We came upon the Linger boys, Dale and Dave, who were out looking over the situation. Dale was in Nettie's class, Dave one ahead of me. Daddy got them to help launch the boat. I really liked it when they grabbed me under the arms and lifted me in. I was sure Nettie would die that she missed such a chance with that adorable Dale Linger.

Daddy used an oar to paddle us along, and soon we were in a neighborhood of row houses with water up around the porches.

"Mr. Beeson, Mr. Beeson," someone called out. Daddy paddled the boat toward the voice.

"That's Mrs. Denniston, I think," he said to me. I now had an oar and was trying to paddle on the other side of the boat, without much success. I'd put my oar down in the water and try to pull it back, but I kept hitting things underwater sticking up out of the ground. In the dark, it was impossible to tell what was where. What finally worked best was putting the oar straight down through the three or four feet of water and using it as a pole to push us along. By the time we reached her porch, Mrs. Denniston was nearly hysterical.

"Will you please look at what this is doing to our property? The foundation is sopping wet and soggy. The whole front of the house is going to collapse. When is the township going to do something about this creek so it doesn't overflow? Mr. Beeson, you said you were going to do something about this. What have you done?"

She was screeching like my mother did when she got really mad. Daddy pulled the boat over to the house and stepped, as gingerly as a man his size could, onto the porch. Mrs. Denniston, who had now been joined by her husband and two small children, shook Daddy's hand. I grabbed onto the Denniston's porch railing to keep the boat from drifting away.

"Mrs. D, I don't think your house will collapse, really," I could hear Daddy say. "We've been working on this, but we have a long way to go. I'll get the township engineers to come out to inspect everyone's foundations once the storm is over."

A group of neighbors waded out in water up to their thighs to see who was in the boat. One of the men started telling me how impressed he was with Daddy's heroism. First he'd campaigned in hip boots to clean up the stream and now he'd come to see a flood firsthand in a boat.

"But isn't this *just great?*" I responded, still thrilled by the adventure. "Who ever thought I'd be in a boat in the middle of Radnor Street Road?"

Just at that moment, Daddy happened to be stepping back into the boat. "Donnan! It is *not* great," he remonstrated. "Can't you see how upset these people are, how much damage is being done? This isn't fun for anyone." He turned to the man I'd been talking to and apologized for my insensitivity.

"It *is* tough when all this water starts toward the only house you have," the man said, "but she didn't mean anything bad, Mr. Beeson."

As we paddled away, Daddy turned to me. "Dee, you've got to think about what these people are going through. They're afraid their houses are going to fall down. You don't tell them, *This is great.* You've got to learn to be sympathetic. Just try to imagine, if you can." His upset put a damper on the moment, but it was a lesson that would stay with me all my life.

The spring I was set to graduate from Penn State, my father's political future was threatened. He'd been in office for ten years, long enough for a groundswell for change to grow and an opponent to emerge. Since being a commissioner was clearly more important to him than his day job as a steel executive, he was worried.

I didn't know what my future held either. I'd accelerated my course work so I could graduate a semester early and get on with my life, whatever that would be. What I really wanted to do was join the Peace Corps, and I went home for a weekend to advance that idea.

"Have you ever heard of Dar es Salaam?" I casually inquired at dinner, thinking my parents would be impressed that I could pronounce Tanganyika and knew its capital city. But when I suggested I was interested in going there as a Peace Corps volunteer, Mother was suddenly full of fear about my safety and health. I could have disregarded that, as I did most of her concerns, but Daddy's advice struck me.

"What I'd worry the most about, if I were you, is this," he began. "So you go away for two years and you come back. Who's going to hire you? How are you going to explain away those two years as a volunteer? You're twenty-one now. You can't expect people to put up with this kind of thing when you're starting a career," he said.

A *career?* At the time, Peace Corps was brand new, and neither of us could have known how many career doors would be opened rather than closed for volunteers. But it had never even occurred to me that I would be starting a *career*. Although I'd begun dating my good friend, David Runkel, at the *Daily Collegian*, my goal after graduation was a job, an interesting one if possible. No telling when (or if!) I might get married. But

now, in the face of Daddy's concern about my career, Peace
Corps began to evaporate.

Not long after I was back at school for the final few weeks
of life in the dormitory before graduation, I received a rare
daytime call from my father.

"My campaign is heating up. I could use you here to keep
things going while I'm at work. We need a new brochure, press
releases, signs and buttons. Neighborhood meetings have to be
organized . . . You could do all that after you graduate. What
do you think?"

I was taken aback. Yes, I knew how to do all those things.
I'd already done some of them before and overheard Daddy
doing the rest. And the experience would be good. But was
working for your father's political campaign any more of a
career enhancer than being a Peace Corps volunteer?

"Daddy, that sounds good, but I think I need to get a *real*
job, don't you?"

"You'll get a job," he said enthusiastically. "You'll have time
to go into the city to look for a job while you're doing this, and
still have the jump on all the June graduates."

As he spoke, I could feel acceptance building in me. I was
needed. There was a place for me, a familiar place. I could return
home as someone my father thought was valuable, someone
who could be trusted to say the right thing—not how great it
was when people's foundations were crumbling.

After two interviews with A.Q. Mowbray at the American
Society for Testing and Materials in Philadelphia, I landed a
job as a technical editor. My father was much more excited
than I was; this meant I'd be employed but still able to work
on the campaign. He was particularly delighted we could drive
together, me at the wheel, into the city everyday. I was glad
to have a job, if not dreading a little the notion of spending

my days copy editing dense text about the tensile strength of titanium used in supersonic transport.

Four months into my career, my status changed dramatically. David Runkel proposed during one of my visits to him on the opposite end of the state. This new prospect of getting married fueled my work, and my ASTM paycheck financed my trips to see him, as well as a modest savings account. My life was actually moving forward.

When Election Day finally came around, I took the day off to work at the polls. My job was to check people off as they came to vote, try to keep track of who hadn't voted so we could pick them up and drive them to the polls, and to count the votes of those we could be pretty sure had voted for my father. As the polls were closing, we knew it would be close. When everything was tallied, Daddy had lost by eleven votes.

I couldn't get over feeling responsible. If this was how campaign managers felt, I didn't ever want to do it again. Daddy's response was more philosophical—he'd given it his all, and the people either hadn't listened to him, or the other guy had spent more money on his campaign than we had.

I spent the following weekend writing thank-you notes to everyone who'd been involved and dropping them off with miniature boxes of Whitman Samplers. I'd convinced Daddy they'd be great souvenirs and leave everyone with a good taste in their mouth for him. Besides, I loved how cute they were—yellow with a pattern of sweet little flowers cross-stitched around the edge. For a long time, one of those little boxes from the campaign held a prominent place on my dresser. Every now and then I'd open it to make sure I hadn't forgotten to eat the last chocolate.

A few weeks before our November wedding, I woke up with a pain in my stomach so severe that I couldn't reach over to turn off the alarm. Even when I doubled myself up, knees to my chin, the pain did not diminish. The alarm kept ringing. Incensed, my mother stormed into my room. "Why haven't you turned it off? What's the matter with you?" she wanted to know.

"Mom, I'm sick. I can't move."

She reached over to my forehead. "You don't have a temperature. You'll be better once you get moving. Come on," she said, grabbing my arm to help.

I managed to get out of bed, but I was bent in half at the waist, a shuffling right angle. My mother put one hand on my lower back and sort of guided me along the hall to the bathroom.

"I can't go to work like this. What do you think is the matter?" I asked her.

"You'll be okay. It's probably a bad case of premarital nerves," she said.

This was not a malady with which I was immediately familiar, but later as I lay in bed, it dawned on me what she was talking about. I was totally mortified.

Midday the phone rang. I managed to hobble into my parents' room and catch it by the eighth ring. It was my father. "How're you feeling, honey?"

"The pain's not as sharp, but I still can't straighten up all the way," I said, holding on to the bedside table to steady myself.

"Well, if you get on the 12:35 into the city, you could still get a half day of work in," he suggested. The thought of going to work had definitely not occurred to me. But guilt crept over me for having given up even half a day's work. Daddy always talked about "backsliders," people who made excuses for not working regularly. And pain was never a good excuse—he regularly told the story of how he played the second half of a football game with a broken finger held together with electrical tape. I didn't want to be a backslider in Daddy's eyes.

"Okay, Daddy. Okay. I'll get dressed. I'll call you from my office," I said, futilely trying to straighten up.

Stepping onto the stairs of the train, I was so bent over I nearly smudged my nose on the next step. I could actually smell the dirt. The conductor wanted to know what was the matter. "Just a stomach ache," I said, looking up at him. By evening, I was pretty much cured. Daddy was right—the show must always go on.

By the time the pain came back again, David and I were married and living 450 miles across the state in a small town. David was out covering a meeting for the newspaper, and this time the pain was even more excruciating than before. It hurt to talk. When my brand new husband got home, I whispered to him that I'd had a recurrence of premarital nerves. I was curled up in the tightest ball I could make.

David immediately called Dr. Smith. He told me to take a few aspirin.

At 6:00 a.m. after a sleepless night, I heard someone banging on our door. Who could be here at this hour? It was Dr. Smith, and he wanted to see my stomach. He'd worried about it all night. After a quick exam, he put his arm under my shoulder and gingerly moved me up into a sitting position.

"I'm going to take you with me to the hospital, Deedie. You've got acute appendicitis, and we have to move fast."

When the surgery was over and I was recovering, the doctor and the surgeon came in to talk.

"There was evidence of at least three other attacks of appendicitis," they said. "You're lucky to be alive. Even if you have a high threshold, it's hard to imagine putting up with the kind of pain you must have had."

They went on to tell me that in addition to acute appendicitis, they'd found I had a severe case of endometriosis, which had destroyed one ovary and part of the other. I'd never heard of endometriosis, nor ever given a thought to my ovaries. As I tried to assess what all this might mean, they went on, patiently explaining how the endometrium is the lining of the uterus, and sometimes it breaks away and attaches itself to other organs, causing great pain and unusual bleeding.

"My parents thought the pain would go away once I was married," I said, struggling to stifle a sob.

"Hmm. That's interesting," Dr. Smith said politely. "But now what's important is that you get started on your family if you plan to have children. Your chances of getting pregnant are slim and going to be slimmer the longer you wait. So let's get you well and get started," he said, patting my hand before he left my bedside.

I heard Daddy in the hallway before I saw him. I couldn't believe he was here. He was asking the nurse her name and whether or not she knew how I was and where I was. He told her that he and my mother were really concerned about me and needed the staff's help to get me better. He sounded like he was on a campaign stop. It turned out he'd chartered a plane to come the minute David called to say what happened and how sick I was. I'd never known him to do such a thing.

"Hey, Dee," he said, striding toward my bed, carrying a big bag. "Let's get you up and out of here." He gave me a kiss on my cheek. All I could do was cry, which made my stomach hurt and my throat sore.

"I can't get up yet. It hurts too much," I said. "I fainted and threw up when they sat me up earlier. Please, just let me lie very still and not die. Have you ever had appendicitis, Daddy?"

He planted his hand on mine. "That's what my brother Buzzy had," he said. "But you're not going to die." We'd always heard about Buzzy dying when he was only seven, but never before this moment did I know it was from appendicitis.

"The doctors said I could have died, like Buzzy did," I said, the tears starting anew.

"But you're not going to, Donnan. We know that for sure," Daddy said, leaning down to kiss my forehead.

Later that week, after Daddy had gone back home and I was still in the hospital, I woke up to a strange sensation. Emerging from a deep sleep, I slowly became aware of someone else's hands on my fingers. As she came into focus, I saw a nurse working to unclench my hands, finger by finger, from the ironclad grip I had on the sheets.

"You're never going to get well, honey, until you relax. Let's get these fingers straightened out. There. See if you can't let all that energy you were putting into making a fist go into getting well."

I had a new focus. Keeping my hands open helped release all the tension I had been harboring. With my hands open, I could replace embarrassment and shame for not responding to my pain, with appreciation for my courage. With my hands open, I could forgive my parents for ridiculing the pain and replace my resentment with an understanding of the limitations of a life lived with a stiff upper lip. With my hands open, I could replace my grief over maybe not being able to bear my own children with anticipation for children we might adopt.

❧

When we moved from tiny Franklin, Pennsylvania, to big Baltimore, we were different, and so was the world around us. We had an infant son, Marshall, to whom I'd given birth just two months earlier. Leaders of the civil rights and anti-war movements were our leaders. Taking to heart Martin Luther King, Jr.'s challenge to build a color-blind world, we joined others in integrating and working to improve the neighborhood near Johns Hopkins University. We were regulars at demonstrations and marches. The American Friends Service Committee was around the corner from us, and we went there on a regular basis for organizing meetings. The hands that had unclenched during my hospital ordeal now reached out to people who reminded me of the folks I'd met in my own living room during my father's political career. The persuasive powers I'd employed to educate people about the necessity for clean streams during my father's campaign, I now used to persuade people to help end the war in Vietnam.

I felt like I was doing what came naturally, considering my background, but my parents couldn't understand how someone raised by them could abandon traditional values and beliefs for what they called the radicalism of the day. They were appalled at where we lived and what we stood for, and they told us so. They couldn't understand why we didn't move when the fires from riots sent smoke throughout our house and brought National Guardsmen with bayonets to patrol our neighborhood. They thought children raised Republican should stay Republican.

A long time had passed with little or no contact between us. Then one day Daddy called to say he'd be in Baltimore on business and wanted to take David and me out to dinner. I was cautiously optimistic about the chance to see him without my mother present. Maybe he and I would find ourselves on the same side, just as we had been in the past.

He met me at the Chesapeake, a restaurant David and I could never afford. David was coming later, so just the two of us were there, face to face. I had recently found out I was pregnant with our second child. He told me he was looking forward to seeing her. "A girl, like you, maybe?" he said. By that time he'd had a few drinks. Even though I was pregnant, I probably had one or two myself.

"Will you *please* tell me why you persist in doing all these things that are only making trouble?" he launched in. I knew he was talking about our anti-war activities.

He and I hadn't ever discussed the war in Vietnam. We'd already been estranged from my parents by the time David and I had gotten deeply involved in protest marches, the Vietnam Moratorium, and community education about the war.

"Daddy, we're *not* making trouble. We're trying to make things better," I began. "And here's why: You taught me. You told me. Every chance you got you made sure I knew how important it was to know things, to be educated, to *do* something. How could I not do anything when all the most respected educators in the country—the president of Yale, the president of *Harvard*, for God's sake—all of them are saying we have to go another way, a new way?" Tears streamed down my face. I could feel red blotches coming out on my neck and chest. My voice was raised, shaking. "The war is *wrong*. We've been lied to. Daddy, you taught me to be like this, can you understand that? Can you remember how you felt when you first discovered our creek was polluted, and you realized you had to get everyone to do something about it? That's how I feel now."

My father put his large hand on top of mine. I could see his big blue veins, so pronounced, and his crooked finger that had once been fixed with electrical tape. I didn't know what was going to happen next. He looked down at his plate, then lifted his head and our eyes met. Leaving the weight of his hand on mine, he kept gently patting, saying nothing.

I sat straight up, pulled my hand out and gently placed it on top of his. It looked so small on top of his huge hand.

"This is the moment, Daddy. This is the moment when you finally can hear why I do what I do. You were elected township commissioner because you believed there had to be a change. Don't you see, you are my model, my hero?"

Our eyes were locked, and I thought I saw tears forming in his eyes. *Had I made my father cry?* Suddenly I felt like I might have done something wrong. Maybe I shouldn't have come on so strong.

Our desserts arrived, and my father pulled away to order another drink. Not long after, David arrived. "What have you been talking about?" he asked.

"Your wife's been making a pretty good case . . . . " my father said, looking over at me, "for this time in history." Our moment had come, and none too soon.

A few months later, my father died on his way home from work—before his granddaughter Lucy was born, but after he knew his legacy was in place.

CHAPTER FOUR

My Ringmaster

My brother Bill was born with a natural vision for grand things. He could invent Niagara Falls from the kitchen faucet. When I was five and he was twelve and our family lived in Pittsburgh, Pennsylvania, my brother transformed the entire neighborhood gang into a one-day circus. A sepia photo shows about thirty-five kids gathered around a handsome boy in tails, our ringleader, ringmaster and star of the day. I am in the second row on the left, Bill's little sister relegated to the less-than-glamorous role as mother of the bride for the Tom Thumb wedding that would be the culminating act. The shoulders of a dark brown velvet jacket droop down near my elbows, a long dark skirt trails in the grass. I'm holding a big pocketbook under one skinny arm. Under the black straw hat is a pathetically sad face with dark circles under the eyes.

Only hours before I had been sent half a block to Abey's Corner Market to get sugar. On the way home, the precious wartime ration book I had been entrusted with somehow went its own way. The fury of my mother's remonstrations was matched only by the storm she turned on my father and brother when they suggested she was being too harsh on me. I sobbed until I had the hiccups and thought I would never be happy again and, worst of all, that I wouldn't be able to be in the circus. My role that day would end up being my last in any of Bill's extravaganzas, which he produced in one form or another throughout his life.

Bill's life as a teenage impresario continued when we moved the next year across the state of Pennsylvania. Soon his Oak Lane Players were putting on productions that rivaled those of the local high school, as well as those of the Footlighters, the community theatre our parents acted in regularly. While never cast in any of these productions, this little sister had been determined to make her presence known. During the early days of this youthful troupe's life, I sat in the front row of every performance gesturing wildly, giggling, tapping my foot, putting my hands over my face and playing peek-a-boo with the actors. Bill finally told my parents he wanted me banished.

Bill's friends Gordon, Mudsy, Bill Webb, Tommy and Jules were regulars in Oak Lane Player productions. By the time they were high school seniors, their parents had all decided that performances were taking too much time from everyone's studies and called a halt to operations. Or so they thought. The young thespians went underground—literally—into the Connally's garage under their house, emerging months later with Cornelia Otis Skinner's "Skin of our Teeth." While everyone else thought they'd stopped rehearsing, I knew about it because I'd secretly read the letter from Samuel French, Inc. giving them permission to perform the play.

In fact, I'd been regularly inspecting Bill's room on the sly over the previous four years. Like me, he had a huge marble-top mahogany bureau, but his looked like an advertisement for an orderly life. On the left side, next to his wallet, change, and keys (if he was home), there would be a stack of letters from the many people with whom he corresponded. Aunt Margaretta's were especially interesting—long letters about music and opera in her wide scrawling hand, on short pieces of writing paper from the American Stationery Company in Peru, Indiana. She reported on every concert she attended or new recording she'd heard, and each summer she would come with Russell, her chauffeur, and pick up Bill to take him to the Tanglewood Music Festival in the Berkshires. A number of the letters I read were rejection notices from various publications, many from *The New Yorker*.

On the far right side, there would always be a neat stack of sealed letters ready to mail, which I regretted not being able to read, and the playbills and programs from events he'd attended recently on the far right end. At least fifty books would be arranged in small piles around the room. Some from the library, some new that our Granny had bought through the Book-of-the-Month club, some he'd bought himself from Miss Virginia at the Book Shelf, and some from the endless shelves of books lining our living room. On his desk a play was usually in the works, and often a short story or some poems were waiting for polish.

The most dominant feature of the room, after its orderliness, was a massive bed with a carved headboard that went nearly to the ceiling. When you lay in it, which I sometimes did while reading Bill's writing or mail, the headboard creaked and seemed to lean toward the footboard. This didn't worry me, because I had recently done a report on the Leaning Tower of Pisa. Experts said it would never fall.

When Bill left the house for Bowdoin College, I found that being the devilish little sister was a far more comfortable role for me than that of awkward teenager supposedly on the threshold of maturity. No longer able to feed off Bill's life, I had to face the hard reality of creating my own. Advice came at me from all the usual quarters, most of it negative: *With your figure, you shouldn't wear that ridiculous pink angora sweater. You should never have let them cut your hair that short. You should wear make-up. You'll never get anywhere at this rate.* (That one in response to a report card with all B-pluses.) In the face of this never-ending litany, I couldn't imagine what I would or could become, or even, was. It never occurred to me that I too could have an orderly dresser like Bill's and aspire to be a writer or make interesting things happen.

Like a dutiful older brother, Bill did provide me with my debut into dating by fixing me up with a friend of his, for the Winter Follies Weekend at Bowdoin. I was to be Peter Shackley's date at the Psi Upsilon house. My parents had volunteered to be chaperones at the Beta Theta Pi house, Bill's fraternity. Peter Shackley was thin, blonde and earnest, maybe a little handsome but certainly not charming, and he had no idea at all what to do with me. I was, after all, only fifteen and little help since my only other date had been to the afternoon movies with Teddy Connally when I was twelve. I noticed right away that Peter and I were often introduced along with other couples, so I would wait for one of the other girls to say she was a junior at Wellesley or Smith, and then I'd say, "I'm a sophomore" and hope they wouldn't ask me what I was majoring in at Radnor High School.

At some point in the evening, Peter Shackley suggested we go to Bill's fraternity house to see what was going on there. I was relieved. This would be more familiar territory, since I'd already met many of my brother's friends, and my parents were there. We'd barely gotten in the door when someone told us that the party had been taken over by two older people who were standing on a table downstairs singing dirty songs. I knew immediately who those two older people were. Mortified, I tried in vain to steer Peter away.

"My parents used to live in West Virginia, that's where they learned all these songs," I whispered to him as we descended the steps to the tune of "Rye Whiskey." My father stopped singing when he saw me come into the room. "C'mon, Dee, you know this one. C'mon up here." I wildly waved no and turned my head to the wall, just as those gathered turned their heads to see who he was talking to. "Donnan, dear. Come on over," my mother added in a voice she reserved for the public, parties and drinking. Thankfully, they took my cue for once. Daddy helped my mother down from their perch and they came over to talk to us.

When the evening was over, I retired to Professor Frederic Tillotson's home, where I was to spend the night. In the hallway my brother and his girlfriend Carol, my roommate, were kissing good night. I climbed the stairs to our assigned sleeping space in the garret of the third floor. The skin of a brown bear had been provided to protect me from the freezing Maine night. It was so heavy I could hardly turn over.

Some time in the wee hours, I awoke, needing to relieve myself of the substantial amount of orange juice mixed with beer I'd consumed at the party. I extricated myself from the bear's embrace and, clad only in my blue flannel Lanz nightgown, began creeping toward the bathroom. I felt my way along the dark hallway, down the steep garret steps, and started down the broad stairs to the second floor. On the landing, I tripped over a body and fell. Sprawled on the floor next to it, I opened my eyes to find myself face to face with my brother. I whispered loudly in his ear, "Bill, wake up, it's time to go to bed!" He was gone, absolutely immobile.

What was wrong with him? I shook him. I tickled him, poked him, moved his head back and forth. What if he was dead?

He certainly was cold enough to be dead. A distorted sense of responsibility took over. I had to get him out of the way so my roommate could go to the bathroom when she got up without trampling on him. My mother and father were staying at the Beta house, and they should probably be notified that their son had died in the hallway of Professor Tillotson's house. But how would I reach them without waking everyone else up?

Desperately acting on the chance that I could still revive him, I stole down the steps to the kitchen and pried out a tray of ice from the freezer. Shaking from either cold or fear, I emptied the tray in the sink, took a few cubes in my hand and scrambled back up the stairs. I began rubbing Bill's face with them. No response . . . . well, maybe a flicker of his eyes.

Sobs welled up in me, wracking my shivering body. I ran back downstairs to the kitchen, thinking perhaps if I put his hand in a bowl of ice water, he'd come to, the same way we used to wake people up at camp by putting their hands in *warm* water. On my way down, I stubbed my toe on the last step and yelled "Ouch," which must have wakened Professor Tillotson, because he was standing over Bill when I returned from the kitchen.

"My brother seems to be dead," I said, tears escaping in a rush. "Shouldn't we call my parents?"

"I think he just needs to sleep it off," the professor said, putting his arm around me. *Could one sleep off death?*

"Why don't you go get the bear skin for your brother, and I'll get you another blanket," he suggested. Dragging the bear off the bed took supreme effort. Struggling down the steps together, I feared the bear's weight would overtake me.

Back in bed, I couldn't stop shaking. What if he really was dead? Had I blown the opportunity to save my brother's life? How did I get such an important role in what seemed like a play but was real? The wait for dawn was endless.

The next morning the Beta Theta Pi's offered up their traditional after-party menu, a punch containing the remnants of all the leftover liquor bottles. I watched my brother join those consuming it enthusiastically.

"Bill, shouldn't you be careful not to get drunk again?" I asked.

"Mind your own business, little Sissie," he flared, stomping away.

By the time Bill was fifty-four, he was living alternately on the streets of New York and at the Westside YMCA. Besides his job as a writer for *US News and World Report*, he possessed a few changes of clothing and a strong desire for his next drink. Rarely losing hope that there was something I could say or do to fix him, I tried promises, threats, heartfelt letters . . . . anything I could think of to convince him I wanted him to sober up and be normal. He was my only brother after all, a strong critic but also a tap root for our life together. I cherished him, but not when he was drunk. And I felt helpless.

One day the phone call came. Bill had been admitted to the emergency room and was hovering near death. Over the next few weeks, however, as I and other family members paid daily visits to the hospital, Bill showed no signs of dying. The doctors were astonished with his remarkable comeback. Somehow reluctant to acknowledge the powerful role alcohol played in his situation, they said only that heart disease and emphysema from many years of smoking would require him to have oxygen around the clock for the rest of his life.

The big question was where would he go after the hospital? As long as he was likely to be sick *and* drunk, I was not ready to take responsibility for him—nor was my sister, nor was his daughter, nor his wife with whom he hadn't lived for years. Ultimately, we all converged at the side of his bed and told him right out he was an alcoholic—just like our mother and our father and both our grandmothers. We told him we loved him and cared about him and knew he could recover. And if he would go through a month-long treatment program, David and I would take care of him until he could go back to work. If he wouldn't go into treatment, we couldn't do another thing for him . . . . *ever*.

"I'm not an alcoholic. I'm just having a hard time right now," he parried. His daughter Avery screamed and cried, "I need you to be my father." We repeated our promise. He said he'd think about it. "I don't plan on dying," he said.

In his twenty-eight days of treatment, Bill discovered he had a lot in common with men and women he would otherwise never have deigned to meet. They were his bridges to a new life, free of alcohol and tobacco. His absolute determination, his discipline and his amazing conviction inspired every one with whom he came in contact, patients and staff alike.

The dresser in Bill's room at our house was soon an orderly array of letters and papers. From the doorway, I smiled at the familiar stacks of books, along with the blue Twelve Step book, on his bedside table. Bill's contribution to our household was as babysitter for our ten-year-old daughter Sara. She was devoted to him and rapidly became the only one in the house who knew how to fix his oxygen tank when it whistled. The cord to the tank trailed them through the house as he cooked with her in the afternoons and helped her with her homework. He joined her on the bus to ballet class, carrying four hours worth of oxygen in a tank on his shoulder. And in his own unique way, he helped her get through those embarrassing stages of adolescence.

"What exactly are we training those bosoms to do?" he asked her when she acquired her first "training" bra.

While some days were easier than others for Bill, never did he show any disposition toward another cigarette or one more drink. Resigned to being on oxygen and probably on disability for the rest of his life, he began researching a healthy place where he could live. San Luis Obispo, California, seemed to be a lively arts community. It had a university, an Episcopal church and a daily newspaper for which he could possibly write.

The blue nylon gym bag *US News* had given him for Christmas was plenty big to hold all of Bill's possessions for the trip to his new life. Everything else he owned had been dumped on a street in New York when he'd first been evicted. As we drove to the airport, I asked him, for reasons I still cannot fathom, how many changes of underwear he had. When he said two, we turned around and went back to buy two more. I guess it was hard for me to imagine my brother who had so much owning so little.

The night before he left, I'd found a small package next to my place at the table.

"Bill, this is not the time for presents," I called out to the kitchen, where he was serving up what would be our last dinner together for a while.

"Hurry and open it. You'll love him," he called back from the kitchen.

Inside the package was a royal blue china box with an elegant Dalmation sitting on top. Years before, we'd had to put down our beloved Dalmation, Leonard Cohen. No one had grieved more than Bill. Now he was returning "Len" to me. The accompanying note was brief.

"Thank you, Sissie. All my love, Bill."

The people who met Bill on arrival in his new town, he wrote, were from the American Lung Association's Short Pants Club—as in panting for air. They showed him around town and helped him find an apartment. Within a week he had an address of his own and had hired a student to be his driver. Within a month or two, he had a small and smart coterie of friends. By the end of the first year, he had a part-time job doing art and theatre reviews for the paper, had spearheaded the formation of the County Drug and Alcohol Abuse Council, and was on the board of the Arts Center. Over the next fifteen years, Bill became well-known throughout the mid-coast, wrote several books, produced and acted in a number of productions and lived happily in a small house he slowly but surely filled with beautiful books, art, music and friends.

On the day my brother intended to die, those who had converged at his bedside fifteen years earlier returned. The hospice attendant told us that even though he appeared to be sleeping most the time, we should still talk to him. Hearing is the last sense you lose, she said, so we should use this time to share any important messages we might have for him. We took turns telling him all the ways his life had enriched our own. I told him I would never have had the nerve to take on challenges in the way I had without his example, and that his comeback had inspired me with the courage to do whatever I set out to do. His nephew Colin told Bill how he had inspired in him his love of art. Lucy thanked him for introducing her to poetry and Scrabble, even though he never let her win. His daughter Avery asked him please to open his little beady blue eyes just one last time so she could see them and kiss them.

Avery and I stayed when everyone else left. We were napping next to Bill on his bed when suddenly his hand grabbed mine, tight. I jumped up in time to see that his eyes were open, focused squarely on Avery.

"Avery, look, he heard you. His eyes are open," I said.

"Thank you, Daddy," she said, smothering his forehead and face with an avalanche of kisses. Then for an awkward moment we didn't know what to do. Even though it had been a month since Christmas, I asked Avery what his favorite carol was. Together we began singing "It Came Upon a Midnight Clear."

We thought the nurse was coming in to tell us to stop singing in the middle of the night. Instead, she told us she could see from the monitors that death was near. It was just about midnight.

As we waited in silence, I remembered my conversation with that same nurse at the beginning of the day.

"He's been coming up with some pretty wild stories," she'd said. "He just tried to tell me that he was a ringmaster in the circus."

Avery and I looked straight at her and chimed in unison, "He *was* a ringmaster."

CHAPTER FIVE

Sterling Silver

Through the crepe-thin layers of my junior bridesmaid's dress, I could feel the warmth of the curb where I sat sobbing. It was the day of my sister Nettie's wedding. She was eighteen, had been away for one year of junior college, and now this. Everyone had gathered to see her off with her Air Force Officer husband on a perfect June day in 1956. The newlyweds had dashed through the rain of rice and settled into a sleek convertible someone had lent for the occasion. I watched through tears as they drove down the tree-lined driveway.

Surprising as a crack of lightning on a hot summer night, emotion had struck me down. What made me cry so? Was it because of losing my sister's presence in my life? Or the realization that I would now be the only one at home? The child.

The youngest of seven bridesmaids in my sister's wedding, I was the only one wearing flat shoes. At fifteen, I was plenty old enough for heels, but I didn't have the nerve. Besides, my feet were swollen from the poison ivy I'd gotten while hiking barefoot in the woods.

For Granny, it seemed clear that I'd meant to get poison ivy. Her vision of perfectly-shod bridesmaids was ruined. By me and my lavender satin flats. Granny had planned every last detail of this extravagant and elaborate wedding. The date, location, dresses, food, bridesmaids. She even influenced the choice of groom, a man from a Naval family whom Nettie had first met when he was a student at nearby Valley Forge Military Academy. Granny had coached Nettie closely throughout the romance—what she should wear for which event, what to wear when she went to meet her future parents-in-law, how often she should write letters. She had steered Nettie perfectly through it all with a sure and confident hand—until I stumbled in with poison ivy.

"I'm disappointed in you, Dee," Granny said when I showed her my swollen, blistered feet.

"What difference does it make what shoes she wears?" Nettie stepped in. I perked up, glad for her support. Then she added, "You know Donnan. She always has something wrong with her."

Contrast defined our early years as sisters. At fourteen, Nettie could have been mistaken for a starlet; I at the same age could have been a poster girl for uncomfortable adolescence. My mouth was so full of stainless steel orthodontia my lips protruded. My leg was in a plaster cast for months. I had a dash of pimples and a Lilt home permanent gone awry. I often despaired of ever achieving anything close to Nettie's beauty, even though there was a lot of effort to point me in the right direction. One day I overheard Granny saying, "Don't you think Donnan's swimming will be good for her baby fat?" That gave me hope.

The four years that separated us in age were more like a hundred when it came to how we were perceived by almost everyone. For the essential dance lessons, Nettie was sent to

Mrs. Chew's Dancing Assemblies, to which she would be driven sheathed in yards of sparkling net, kept warm by a long turquoise velvet coat. Mrs. Chew's was down the Main Line in neighboring Merion, and only a few of the girls from Wayne went there, which made me believe you had to be beautiful or rich to qualify. I, on the other hand, was sent to Mrs. Hill's dancing school right in our own town.

There I was supposed to learn the niceties of social convention and ballroom dancing. The method used to obtain a dancing partner was one I found so excruciatingly painful that I spent more time in the cloak room than on the dance floor. The girls were lined up on one side of the room, the boys on the other. When Mrs. Hill, who once danced on the New York stage, gave the signal, the boys would dash across the floor to choose a partner. I in my hand-me-down evening gown, was rarely chosen. The un-chosen usually spurned Mrs. Hill's suggestion that we dance with each other and repaired to the cloak room.

Nettie was accustomed to being chosen for things. The lead in the play or in the ballet. Or her paintings chosen for a show at the art center. Or for dates with boys whose homes Granny said were good. The summer I traded championship swimming for a cast on a broken leg, Nettie had been chosen to go to Germany as an exchange student. While she was busy charming her German family, I was learning to use crutches as my primary source of transportation.

Her return from Europe that summer marked a turning point in our relationship. As would be expected, she brought back gifts for each of us. Granny got a blue and white ceramic pitcher. Mother and Daddy got liqueur glasses. Brother Bill got a German libretto for his favorite opera. To me she presented an exquisite sterling silver jewelry box with its own key. In awe,

I unlocked it and carefully opened the lid. It was lined with sophisticated black velvet. For me . . .

I could hardly wait to incorporate the beautiful box into my room. I immediately made my way upstairs, careful not to catch the crutches in the carpet and drop my treasure. All the furniture in my bedroom was antique, with relevance to the family's history but little to mine. But this special box was *my own.* I cleared off the marble-topped dresser and placed it in the center, startled by the sudden reflection of the silver's gleam in the mirror. I had one thing valuable enough to put in it—a gold ring with a turquoise. I laid it inside, closed the lid and turned the key. This was the first time I realized that I had inherent value as a sister.

Owning that box made me feel I could actually imagine myself as a grown-up. There would be future treasures that it one day would contain. Besides this silver box, one day I would even have engraved silver of my very own that I would get to polish—not the silver I was *made* to polish in the dining room. When family and friends came to visit, I would say, "Wait 'til you see what Nettie brought me from Germany. C'mon." Up the creaky stairs they'd climb to view the silver box in the middle of my dresser. I secretly hoped that since they worshipped Nettie, the fact that she had given me such a valuable gift would somehow increase their esteem for me.

The rest of my fourteenth summer I relied on the huge dresser mirror to reveal any progress my body might be making toward looking more like Nettie's. Reading *The Diary of Anne Frank* inspired me to do something I'd never done before. I closed the door tight, and undressed. Standing in front of the mirror, I examined my body's reflection as Anne had. This became an ongoing practice of hope until finally one of my inspections revealed evidence that I would be getting breasts after all. I waited eagerly for the right moment to share the news with Nettie.

Still on crutches, I followed her into my room, closed the door and pulled up my tee shirt.

"Look, I said. "Bosoms!"

"Oh, great," she said unimpressed. "I've had 'em since fourth grade. They're a bother, not as much fun as you might think."

"Yeah, maybe. But isn't it great I've got them, finally?" I was going to be in the eighth grade.

"You're going to have to start wearing a bra, you know," she replied.

It turned out Granny had noticed this development as well and had a plan to deal with it, though she kept it a secret until the opportune day.

The cast on my broken leg had been giving me a lot of pain. Mother said she'd had a cast once and it hadn't hurt at all. This seemed to mean mine shouldn't either. After hearing me complain for the third morning in a row, Nettie had come to my rescue.

"Why doesn't she just go back to the doctor?"

"Oh, all right. Stop in Bryn Mawr on your way to the orthodontist then, Donnan," my mother said.

Maneuvering the train trip by myself, on crutches, was a dirty business. Every time I pulled myself up the high steps, or tried to hop down, my dress got a little more soiled. Self-conscious and wet with perspiration, I propelled myself across the threshold of the doctor's office.

One of the nurses laughingly remarked that I looked taller to her. "Maybe you've outgrown that cast and that's why it hurts," she suggested. I felt a momentary lift in my spirits—maybe there was a real reason for my pain.

After a careful measuring of my leg and the cast, it was determined I had indeed grown nearly half an inch in the month since the accident. An ugly ulcer had festered under the pressure.

"Good heavens, girl, you must be really hurting," the doctor said.

I felt redeemed.

Sporting a new plaster cast, with a window carved out for the ulcer's dressing, I was back on the train en route to the orthodontist. Maybe this was my day. Maybe he'd say the braces were ready to come off.

Instead, to my dismay, a new appliance called a "cow catcher" was installed. Spokes from a wire behind the teeth in my upper jaw would keep my tongue from hitting my teeth. Four sets of rubber bands of differing tensile strengths were stretched and strung throughout my oral cavity. Mrs. Hill's dance was coming up in a few days. This new appliance would no doubt safeguard my spot in the cloak room. Not even the minister's son, who sometimes took pity on me, would want to be around all this heavy metal.

Granny's call interrupted the doctor's orientation to my new appliance. The message was that I should stop at Best & Company on my way home. Mrs. Ardern there would have something for me. Best's was the New York store from which Granny had ordered our clothes for years. The Ardmore branch was familiar territory, Mrs. Ardern a trusted ally.

When I crutched my way to her department, Mrs. Ardern presented me with a tasteful brown Best's bag with built-in carrying handle. "Will you be trying one on?" she asked.

I had no idea what was inside. I took a peek, and there they were—six white training bras.

"For me? Oh no," I said, "I don't need to try them on." Fingers perspiring, face flushing and eyes averted, I folded the carrying handles back together. "Thanks, Mrs. Ardern."

It was now so late that the train was filled with fathers on their way home from work. I was sure they were using their x-ray eyes to see through the Best's bag and know there were bras in there for my fledgling breasts. I tried to hide the bag under my crutches.

It was nearly dark when I arrived at the Wayne train station, so I caught the only cab in town for a ride home. Exhausted, I opened the door just as the dinner candles were being lit.

"Where have you *been*?" my mother wanted to know. "What*ever* took so long?"

"Well, first I had to get a whole new cast because I grew out of the old one, and I have a very nasty ulcer the doctor said must be very painful. And then I had to get a cowcatcher," I said, opening my mouth wide so everyone could see.

"What's in the Best's bag?" Nettie demanded.

"She'll show you later, dear," Granny answered.

"What's the big secret in the Best's bag?" my father asked.

"Something just for Donnan. We're not going to talk about it," Granny declared.

Dinner over, Nettie got excused from the table and suggested I join her upstairs when I was done. Moments later I asked to be excused and made my way up the steps on my bottom, too tired to use the crutches for even one more minute. The Best's bag thumped along with me. Nettie was waiting for me in the room she shared with Granny.

"Get your dress off and we'll try one on," she said, opening the bag and pulling out the pile of bras wrapped in tissue paper.

I waited while she took the tags off.

"Do you think they'll fit?" I asked.

"For a while," she said. "This is just the beginning. But you don't want them to grow as big as mine."

"Maybe I do," I said as I sat down on the bed and put one arm and then the other through the straps. Nettie climbed around behind me to fasten the hooks on my latest improvement.

                                 ⤜⤛

The summer I graduated from high school, I was dispatched to Topeka, Kansas to help Nettie with a two-year-old son and soon-to-arrive baby. I was to do babysitting and some of the chores, but mostly I was a tag-along companion. It didn't take long to notice that as a military wife she spent what seemed to be an enormous amount of time doing things that didn't look like much fun. Going to the commissary for food. Worrying about whether or not she had enough money. Traipsing off to various compulsory functions for officers' wives. Was this really the life Granny had planned for her?

It looked distinctly less glamorous than going to Mrs. Chew's, studying art at college, having dates and wearing beautiful clothes. The only spice in Nettie's life seemed to be gossiping with or about the other wives. We never talked about whether she wished she was still in college. She was living a life Granny designed to be the right one. An officer's wife. Mother of beautiful children. Socially active. That had to be correct.

Each day I was there, the gulf between us grew wider. She was pregnant and a mother. I was not. She and her husband talked about sex. It made me blush. I read books, which Nettie didn't have time to do anymore.

Nettie and her husband's agenda for me was to find me a man. I knew I was not remotely interested in being an Air Force wife, but a date might be fun. My brother-in-law seemed to have a particular idea about what that would mean. He enjoyed watching me squirm whenever he said I'd be less uptight once I "got laid."

Unbeknownst to me, this was the plan the night I was set up with Isham for a party at the Officers' Club. Isham was a big sandy-haired guy from Boston who drank his gin and tonic in one gulp. His cheeks got redder as the evening progressed. Dancing and drinks in a smoky dark club led to a midnight ride to the shores of Lake Shawnee. He parked the car and launched his assault on my virginity. The kissing was okay. But this was promptly followed by muscular efforts to take off my white linen sheath. I struggled this way and that around the front seat, on the edge of panic, confident this course of events would not improve my life, no matter what my brother-in-law said.

In a desperate maneuver, I pressed my back against the passenger door and began to kick him away. "Take me home right now," I demanded. Twenty minutes of stony-cold silence later, he returned me, chaste and intact, to my sister's door.

The next morning, Nettie wanted to know if I thought Isham would ask me out again.

"I don't think I'm his type," I told her, trying to sound casual. "Besides he tried to rip my clothes off me."

"You looked so great last night. No wonder. But I bet you're exaggerating," she said. "We'll find out what he thought."

"I don't really care, and besides I'm leaving soon," I responded.

Only much later did the questions begin to arise in me. *What would Nettie have done in the same situation? Did she believe I'd be better off if I "got laid"? Why the hell did she set me up when she knew what Isham was like? Why did she tell my parents I was out all night with "a handsome young lieutenant from Boston"?*

I was beginning to suspect that maybe Granny's grand plan for Nettie was flawed. The question remaining was: *What did that mean for me? About me?*

By the time Nettie returned to live at our parents' house with her three young children, I was happily married to David Runkel, who probably would never have made it onto Granny's list of approved husbands. Even though he was a salt-of-the-earth farm boy, together we seemed to be heading toward a life that, ironically, looked like one with which Granny could be comfortable. We even used her dining room table and served dinners using all the right silver.

Nettie set out to build a new life for herself, a difficult job with no role models (at least in our family) available to her. Her pain and humiliation were suffered in silence. The word "divorce" was rarely uttered, nor was "abuse." The one topic we bonded over when I visited was Granny's influence on our lives, especially now that she was no longer alive.

"I always wonder what Gran would say about having David as my husband," I said on our way to the grocery store one day.

"How could anyone not love David Runkel?" Nettie said. "And look at what we now know about people Granny *did* approve of. Mine may have come from a fine family, but he's certainly not husband and father material," she said.

"What have Mother and Daddy said about your situation?" I asked.

"It's like everything else we never talk about. If you don't talk about it, it's not there," she responded. "I'm sure it would be the same if Granny were still here. Either that or she would find a way to tell me his behavior was my fault," she said.

"Granny may have loved us, but I think she gave us some bum steers, that's what I think," I concluded.

Nettie's future eventually led to a new husband, another child and a move to Memphis. When David and I moved back to Philadelphia, not far from where we grew up, Nettie was eager to visit. She wanted to know if we'd be sending our son Marshall to Mrs. Chew's Dancing Assemblies.

"They're practically next door to you," she said.

"Are you kidding?" I nearly yelled. "Why would I put my child in a situation where he's judged on how he *looks*. I'd never do such a thing, much less pay a lot of money for it."

"It's good for them to learn to dance, and have social skills. Really. You're just visiting your own childhood social insecurities on him, and it's not fair," she countered.

"Nettie, I went through all that business and it never got me anything or anywhere. And besides, you don't need to go through all that claptrap to learn how to dance. All it did was make me more self-conscious than I already was. It's useless. And how dare you suggest I'm depriving Marshall?" Now my voice was raised.

"Oh, Donnan. You're being silly. I'd give anything to be living here and have my kids have the same experiences we did."

"That's where we're different, Nettie, and I'm not ready to say that what Mrs. Chew's and all that offers is even a valid step toward a happy, fulfilled life. I happen to think kids need activities where everyone has a chance. Every minute. No matter what."

"Well, of course, they do," she muttered.

After Nettie left, I spent days ruminating in search of answers.

Nettie had always had what looked right from the outside—the appearance of perfection. Granny had taught her she didn't need to think about happiness or even fulfillment as long as all the items on the "Is This a Correct Marriage?

List" could be checked off. How had I been lucky enough to escape all that? Did all the years I spent being sad that I wasn't beautiful like her or as socially adept actually help steer me toward a meaningful life? I'd always thought I'd had a very difficult childhood, but maybe Nettie's was even tougher.

Nettie returned to college at fifty to get her bachelor's and then her master's degrees, both summa cum laude, and her life changed dramatically. Soon she was working fulltime teaching immigrants at Catholic Charities. Taking part in peace activities. Writing short stories. She complained for the first time about being the only Democrat among her group of friends. She traveled extensively by herself, having amazing adventures in England, France and the Czech Republic. She started painting again. I was amazed, but not surprised, at all she'd become.

When Nettie got her master's degree, her friends had arranged a surprise Graduation Prom for her. They called to ask if I would come. Excited to be going to a prom after all these years—and no longer suffering from "social insecurities"—I'd borrowed a gown from my friend Deba. The bodice was red satin, and the skirt was made with so much bulky, sparkly net I almost had to buy a separate plane ticket for it. I couldn't wait for Nettie to see me decked out like this. Our journey as sisters had come long way from where it began.

I managed to get myself into the dress and over to the party before Nettie arrived. The dress and I took up so much room, people had to make way for me to pass. Everyone was wearing a tiara, and the hostess offered me one. I could hear Granny saying, "Tacky, tacky" under her breath as I placed it on my head.

The door opened and Nettie came in. Everyone cheered. Her kids all rushed to greet her. From the back of the crowd, I could see her scanning the faces to see who all was there. When her eyes met mine, she screamed.

"Donnan! Deedie! What are YOU doing here? Oh my heavens, look at you."

The crowd parted so Deba's debutante dress and I could get to her.

"I wouldn't miss this, my sweet sister. We're so proud of you." My gown and I enveloped her in a hug. "What do you think of my dress? Isn't it sensational?"

"*You're* what's sensational," she said, standing back to take me in. "Thank you so much for coming."

Everyone was silent, watching our reunion. Then the hostess broke in. "Didn't you Philadelphia girls have to get dressed up like this a lot growing up?"

"She did," I said, pointing to Nettie.

"We *both* did, whether we wanted to or not," Nettie said, pointing to me.

CHAPTER SIX

Love, Finally

If I'd had the nerve, I would have asked David Runkel out. But it was 1963, and the most progressive thing I could do was talk about doing such a daring thing with my other friends who were dateless. David and I were students at Penn State, and we spent countless hours together working as editors of the *Daily Collegian*. I loved how smart he was, his indomitable curiosity, and especially his laugh. I was a giggler myself. We seemed to be amused about nearly everything when we were together. After work late at night we both liked to have a chocolate milk shake and a grilled sticky bun at the New College Diner, followed by a smoke. I preferred Pall Malls, he liked Chesterfields.

Late one afternoon just before deadline, the ice finally broke, and it was our fathers who were responsible for the first crack. David had written a blistering editorial, excoriating the Pennsylvania Senate for tucking a $1.2-million provision for scholarships into the University's budget. No one at the University could figure out what scholarships they were talking about. After much investigation, David was able to reveal that the scholarships were a "large patronage package used by the Senators to reward their political friends." Operating in full Editorial-Page Editor style he wrote on: "How outrageous to be playing cheap political games with the state's leading institution of higher education."

I'd interrupted my duties as News Editor to read his piece. I felt my face heating up as I read. *I* had a Senatorial scholarship. (At least my father did for me. It amounted to about $100.00 a term.) I sat for a minute trying to compose my thoughts and then slipped across the City Room into David's office. I closed the door behind me and haltingly confessed my guilt.

When I was done, he looked me straight in the eye and said, "Me too."

After a short discussion about our fathers' various political activities at opposite ends of the state, we decided it would be best to publicly reveal the fact that we were both "scholarship" students. At the foot of the editorial, we inserted:

Miss Beeson and Mr. Runkel are both recipients of Senatorial Scholarships.

Not long after our joint stroke of public integrity, David asked me out. The night before my very last final I would finally have a date with that tall, dark-haired, very blue-eyed wonderful man I had long fantasized about asking out myself.

We went to see "Days of Wine and Roses," during which his hand landed on top of mine and stayed there. It was hard for me to know where I wanted to concentrate—on the movie or on how good it felt to feel the warmth and weight of David's hand. Yet I found the alcoholism portrayed in the movie to be riveting. Those two people could be my parents. *If David knew I came from a home with alcoholic parents, would the hand be removed?*

But for the first time in my life I was seeing that mine was not the only alcoholic home, and oddly that was as comforting as that warm hand.

Alas, my decision to graduate a semester early in order to get on with my Life was cutting short the time I now had with my first serious college boyfriend. Aware of our precarious situation, we covered with alacrity the distance between being good friends and steadies.

Besides our fathers being local Republican operatives, and our families both being Pennsylvania Presbyterians for generations, there was little else about our backgrounds that was similar. When I flew across the state on Allegheny Airlines to spend a weekend at the Runkel farm, I was in totally new territory. I didn't know anything about growing corn or when to pick it. I had never heard of Spring Cleaning as an actual activity. And I hadn't known before then anyone who knew how to make doughnuts.

When David drove across the state in his red Ford Falcon to visit me, he was confronted with my father's conversations about Japanese competition with American steel, how to improve his bridge game, and how to dress to accompany me to functions that required black ties.

Despite the differences, our comfort levels with each other were high, and we shared a sense of how we wanted to enlarge our worlds.

Laughter laced our time with both families. We had declared our love for each other, and people said it showed. For someone like myself whose market price had never been particularly high on the family stock exchange, David's presence caused a surge in my net worth. No one even mentioned the fact that he had a fairly serious stutter or that he'd flunked out of Navy ROTC.

After graduation, David went off to a small Western Pennsylvania town to be *the* city editor, *the* reporter and *the* photographer for the *News Herald.* I continued being a technical editor in Philadelphia. We wrote long letters back and forth about our jobs and our friends, and what we were reading or seeing at the movies. One night I worked up my nerve to write about plans.

I was in desperate need of a future. My life at home was becoming more and more difficult, I wrote to him. My mother was constantly criticizing me, my father was constantly trying to counter her. I'd been really sick, and they'd both said I should ignore it and get into the office to work. I poured out my heart. I even confessed I was reading Erich Fromm's *The Art of Loving* in an effort to understand the importance of love in my life. (When my mother spotted the book on my bedside table, she said I should stop reading "whacko" books like that.) I have to make a plan, I wrote. The letter ended with a thinly-veiled request: "It would be good to know what your plans for yourself are. What are you thinking about for your immediate future?"

For four days after, I nervously anticipated his response—and second-guessed my strategy. *Should I have done such a thing? Was this too forward?* But how come my friends regularly reported on long serious talks about the future with their boyfriends, and David and I never did? I was about to be a bridesmaid for the *fifth* time. I could hardly stand to think about being in another wedding and having to answer all the inevitable questions about my own marital status. Most girls around me knew who they were going to marry by the time they were twenty-two.

Five days after I'd sent my epistle, a fairly fat letter was waiting for me on the sideboard when I came home from work. Eagerly I carried it out to the screened-in porch that stretched across the back of the house. The late afternoon sun lay gently on my mother's huge rose bed just outside the door. Mother was sitting across the room reading a book, having her first drink of the afternoon, and smoking. I plopped down on the wicker rocker where my Granny once held court and began reading, speeding through the letter in search of hope. Instead, there was a recitation of his plans: newspaper, Navy, graduate school, newspaper. Nothing about *us*, except to say we'd talk more that weekend when I went out there, and he was sorry I was unhappy at home.

I read the letter again to make sure I hadn't missed something. My cheeks were growing hotter by the moment. My stomach was churning. I brought the rocker to an abrupt stop, scrunched the letter into a ball, and threw it across the room, yelling "Eahhhhhhhh."

Taffy, our Chesapeake retriever, ran across the porch and dashed back to me with what she thought was a ball. When she realized I wasn't going to throw it for her again, she put her paws on my lap and began madly licking my furious face.

"Donnan, whatever is going on?" my mother asked. "Why are you screaming at six o'clock in the afternoon? Just what do you think the neighbors are going to think?"

I started to cry. She didn't love me. David didn't love me. Only TAFFY loved me. "David's going into the Navy and really doesn't have any plans for us," I said through my tears. "*That's* what's going on and, now hear this, I don't give a good goddamn about the neighbors."

"Watch your language, Lucy Donnan Beeson. You mean he doesn't want to see you anymore?"

Taffy nudged me again, with the letter-ball in her mouth.

"Oh no. Oh no," I said, seething, "He definitely wants to see me. And he thinks it's perfectly all right to have five-year plans that don't include me. But that's not okay with me. I'm calling him right this minute to tell him that," I said, anger roiling now.

"Oh for heaven's sake, Donnan. There's nothing wrong with him having a plan. Just stop being upset. Don't do anything that's going to drive him away. He's a good man, and your father and I respect him. You're lucky to have him around. I wouldn't take the chance if I were you. And besides, it's a long-distance call," my mother concluded.

"Just whose side are you on, anyway?" I shot back. I got up, followed by Taffy, and stomped into the hall where the phone was.

I dialed David's number. The minute he heard my voice, he asked, "Did you, did you, did you get my letter?"

I was sitting at my mother's secretary. I began a nervous doodle among all the old phone numbers and ink spots on the soiled blotter. My palms were slippery on the phone receiver. A lump had appeared unbidden in my throat. Trying to swallow it away, I saw my reflection in the tall glass doors of the desk. Inside were very old books, including a family bible. School pictures of nephews and nieces, neighborhood children and fading news articles were wedged in the wooden fretwork that covered the glass. The face I saw was a stricken one.

"Yes, I got it," I said in a flat voice. "And I have to say I was pretty upset to read all about your plans and not see my name mentioned once." I wanted to say more, but I was running low on nerve, and that lump in my throat was turning into tears. Taffy nuzzled my hand, wanting to be petted.

David's stutter always grew more pronounced when emotions were involved. He was stuttering so much now I was beginning to feel guilty.

"D-d-d-don't worry, D-deedie. We, I mean, we-we, we, yes, we can talk more this, this weekend. When you come, when you come. D-d-d-ad's going to pi-pick you up at the airport," he labored on.

Are you sure I should come?" I asked. I needed proof.

"Of course, of course. Don't, don't don't worry. Please," he said.

"Okay," I said, my shoulders dropping several notches in relief.

"Th-thanks for ca-ca-calling," he said.

"Friday. Two more days," I said, wanting to hold on a little longer.

"'Love you," he said.

"Same," I said and quickly hung up.

⠙

Doc Runkel was called "Doc" because he would have been a vet if the Depression hadn't happened. He was waiting for me at the Pittsburgh airport. This was the third or fourth time he'd picked me up so David wouldn't have to take off work. The airport was part of the territory he covered as a dairy inspector for Meadow Gold. He knew nearly every farm we drove past on the ninety-mile trip North to the Runkel farm. He was also well known at several bars where we stopped on the way. The Bell Bar near Zelienople was my favorite. Dark and a little grungy, its outstanding feature was a collection of every kind of bell imaginable hanging behind the bar. The bartender rang one of those bells for every drink he served. They were great conversational fodder for two people like Doc and myself who led very different lives.

All Friday evening and all Saturday morning, the talk David had promised hovered over us like impending surgery. We visited his high school pal, Tom McFate, in his ancient maroon trailer on Conneaut Lake. We sat around the maple table in his parents' kitchen and heard some of Doc's new jokes. They taught me to play Five Hundred, a favorite family card game. When the lunch dishes were cleared on Saturday afternoon, David announced we were going to Franklin, eighteen miles away, where he lived and worked. I'd been there before, and each time it had painfully highlighted my own questions about my status as an adult in the world. David had his own apartment. He paid his own phone and electric bills. I had never lived independently, and I was desperate to be defined as something other than daughter of Lucy and Bill Beeson.

The one thing I had done toward this end was to shed "Donnan" as my everyday name. Adopting my favorite aunt's name, I became known as "Deedie." No more having to correct people when they invariably called me "Donna." My family didn't exactly welcome the change. "Most people would be proud to have a name like yours, Dee," my mother said.

David had also used college as the chance to change his childhood name. Everyone in Cochranton knew him as "Butch." Whenever I'd talk about "David," I could see them silently translating it back to "Butch."

So that afternoon the former Donnan and the former Butch sat down on an old slightly prickly brown sofa in a second-floor apartment on Buffalo Street in Franklin, Pennsylvania. The late afternoon sun sent long lines of light into the nearly bare living room—a beige shag rug too small for both sets of feet, a wooden chair holding a huge stack of newspapers, an empty beer bottle, a half-full ashtray, and us. David had bought a bottle of port (it was the cheapest thing at the liquor store), and we'd poured ourselves some in juice glasses. Neither of us knew quite how to start this conversation, so we did some kissing instead.

David spoke first.

"I'm, I mean, I'm really, really, really sorry you got the wrong impression from my letter," he said, putting his arm around me and turning me toward him.

I turned to concentrate, my eyes fixed on his. I wanted to hold his hand, but where was it? Oh, around my neck, the other one holding his port, then putting it down.

"B-b-b-but the impor, import, important thing is, you know, you know. It's . . . . will you marry me?"

Would I marry him? Did I hear right? Oh my heavens! I grabbed his hands and leapt off the sofa. Fireworks cascading bursts of blue and gold and pink excitement and joy flooded my mind. We held hands and danced a little jig. And then hugged. Again. And again

"Of course! Of course. I love you, I love you. I love you *so* much, you'll never know how much."

I was frothing with love, literally jumping up and down.

I finally had a destination in life, a role in life, a place to be in life. It was with David Runkel, aka Butch. In that short instant, he'd conferred upon me a sense of worth I had never felt before.

We called everyone from his phone in the hallway, where you had to stand to talk because the chair was in service as a coffee table. When we called my parents, Mother answered. Daddy picked up the upstairs phone.

"We're engaged. We're engaged! Can you believe it?" I was practically shrieking.

"That's wonderful, dear. And you're sure he doesn't feel trapped?" my mother wanted to know.

"Luce, that's not a nice thing to say. Of course he doesn't," my father said, playing his usual rescue role. "Congratulations, Dee. And tell David we said the same to him."

Later that night, David produced a jeweler's box. It held a gold necklace for me, a chain with a pearl pendant. He explained this was meant to be a substitute for a ring until we found one. I didn't take it off until the night before our wedding when he gave me another necklace. Years later David would give me a box to hold both these pledges of love and affection. A miniature chest of drawers, it is painted blue and gold. In the small drawer in the bottom right-hand corner, is my "engagement necklace," a touchstone of that autumn afternoon on Buffalo Street.

❧

On the plane back to Philadelphia the next day, this perpetual bridesmaid was at last making a list for her own wedding. Riding home from the airport with my parents, it became clear that my mother had been making her own list. She opened with the fact that it wasn't going to be easy having another wedding so soon after my brother's. She hoped I didn't have any grandiose ideas.

"You'll have to make an appointment with John Ansley for your engagement photograph. And draft the announcement for the papers," she rattled on. "And Walton's offered to have you wear her dress. I think this is so smart and would save so much money. And what do you think of having a Family Only wedding? You simply have too many friends. Just family makes it much more manageable."

Somehow, it was much more fun being engaged in Franklin.

The Selective Service ended the debate over the size of our wedding and the date. Not long after his proposal, David called, clearly upset. The ramp up to the Viet Nam war was happening. He'd been officially drafted, induction scheduled for November 11. What should he do? He could scramble and try to get into the Navy's Officers' Candidate School. Or, if we got married—in less than six weeks—he'd be ineligible for the draft.

There was no tradition of serving in the military in either of our families. After a remarkably short conversation, in which we decided it would not be un-patriotic if we got married, it was settled. Our wedding would be on November 9, in Wayne,

Pennsylvania. His parents would drive our marriage license to the induction center in Pittsburgh while we had a one-day honeymoon before David returned to work.

While I edited papers on titanium at work, my mother was busy choosing my china and silver patterns, my bridesmaids' dresses and my trousseau. When I wrote to my fiancé to complain about my power being usurped, he wrote back to say how lucky I was to have someone taking care of all the details. With no time left for engraved invitations, my mother wrote formal letters in her tall, elegant script to both extended families, inviting them to be present at the wedding of Donnan and David. David's Aunt Vivian called our number to say she'd received the invitation in error—she knew no one named David or Donnan.

On the day of the wedding, my sister-in-law's dress hung from my bedroom door. My "necessaries" were laid out on my bed the way Granny used to do for me before dancing lessons. The Merry Widow, a contraption of strapless bra, waist cincher and body smoother. Stockings. Lacey pants. One of Granny's hankies. Satin wedding slippers. I had slept my last night as a virgin. My going-away suitcase was packed. I was moving out.

The bathtub was filled with hot water, and I slowly sank into it—into this tub where I'd been a child of six, seven, ten years old. Into this tub in the pink and black bathroom with the grey towels and the dressing table with the chintz skirt that no one ever used. Into this tub where I'd discovered my first pubic hair. Into this tub where the blood from every leg-shaving drained. As I settled into the comfort of familiarity, I began to think about what was next. I knew nothing of what lay ahead, and yet I was going to promise David to be his wife for the rest of my life. The enormity of the commitment landed with a thud on my shoulders. I rounded them toward my breasts and slithered further down in the water. How could anyone make such a promise, knowing so little? The more I thought about it, the less romantic it all seemed. The butterfly population in my stomach suddenly increased exponentially.

A knock at the door.

"Donnan, what's taking so long? Are you okay?" My father. He still had to shave and the other bathroom was in use.

"Daddy, this is a really big thing I'm doing and I'm really nervous," I called.

"It *is* a big thing, Dee. But you know what you're doing." He sounded confident. I ran more hot water and sank back into it. Another knock at the door. "It's Walton. I have something from your father. Is it all right to come in?"

My sister-in-law entered carrying a small snifter of brandy. She said Daddy called it "liquid courage," and said I had to be out in no more than fifteen minutes.

Pictures of me floating down the aisle of Wayne Presbyterian Church on my father's arm show a girl who is in the late stages of fright. No smile. A very pale face. The father of the bride's face is no less grim. When I spotted David at the other end of the aisle, however, I felt a surge of strength and joy I had never known. When we said our vows, edited to remove my promise to obey him, it was with such strong, clear voices that people said they could hear every word, all the way to the back of the church. Nary a stutter was heard.

CHAPTER SEVEN

The Greatest of These

Every time I tried to genuflect, my knees wobbled, my body tilted to one side and I started to giggle. The Monsignor was clearly annoyed. Whenever he opened his mouth to coach me or Tucker on how to do it right, we'd get the giggles all over again. Clearly, Presbyterian girls, even in their early twenties, were somehow not as physically adept as Catholics.

The father of the child inside Tucker's growing belly looked askance at us. This was *his* church, and *his* Monsignor doing *his* family a favor by performing a wedding on a Wednesday morning in September 1963. The ceremony would begin in less than an hour, and Tucker and I had spent most of the brief rehearsal trying not to laugh.

I was wearing the maid-of-honor dress I'd worn for my brother's wedding four months earlier. It had a bustle in the back "to keep the congregation interested," or so we'd been told. Tucker was in a tasteful off-white frock that was getting snugger by the moment. Her pretty dark brown curls fell softly around her face, her blue eyes sparkled.

Tucker and I had been friends since second grade and looked enough alike that we were often mistaken for each other. Dark hair. Blue eyes. Medium build. Thinking I was Tucker, her grandfather would sometimes pull over as I was walking home from school to give me a ride home to see "your grandmother." We'd both laugh with surprise at the error (although I was secretly delighted to be considered pretty enough to be mistaken for Tucker). She was so much a part of our family that the original plan for this wedding got hatched at my parents' house. While her own parents had made it clear they weren't interested in hosting a shotgun wedding, Mother and Daddy willingly participated in the effort to get her married before too much more time elapsed. One evening, Tucker had arrived at our house in tears, needing some support and ideas. At dinner, my father suggested that we all go to the Pocono mountains the next weekend, rendezvous there with the groom, who was in the Army, and get them married. It sounded like a good plan.

Then the phone rang. Knowing it would be the groom, Tucker ran to answer it. We couldn't hear the conversation, although we certainly tried, so when Tucker hung up, eager to hear her report, we waited quietly. And waited.

"Tuck, is everything okay?" I called out.

We could hear the chair being pushed away from the desk. Tucker walked back in and sat down, very glum. We waited. Finally, with her voice cracking, she spoke.

"He says his sergeant cancelled everyone's leave this weekend. The only acceptable reason for leave was if you'd knocked someone up. He can't get away."

Daddy's fork dropped from his hand to the Wedgewood plate that held his half-eaten dinner. "Well, why the hell not? He qualifies, right?" Tucker sobbed. I grabbed her hand.

"I'm really sorry, Mr. Beeson, but I guess it just isn't going to work. He says his family wants a Catholic wedding in

Harrisburg anyway," Tucker offered, regaining her composure. A *Catholic* wedding lay upon the table like a fog over the bay.

"Soon would be a very good idea, don't you think, dear?" my mother asked her, or maybe all of us. The candles flickered as she blew out the cigarette smoke she'd held in as she spoke. "Nettie's friends who've married Catholics have had to promise to raise their children Catholic, you know."

"I know," Tucker answered, resigned to her fate. "The wedding *will* be soon. Maybe next month. But he said I will have to take instruction first. That should be interesting . . . "

Tucker and I had shared a Presbyterian youth. Sunday school, choir and Youth Fellowship. We went through a phase of wishing we knelt in church like our Episcopalian and Catholic friends did. For some reason, kneeling seemed more serious than sitting in a pew. But over all, church was more of a habit than a religion for us, a comfort zone, something we did on Sundays and special occasions, like getting married and dying.

On Sundays sometimes we'd sit near Tucker's grandparents, who had occupied the same spot for more than fifty years. When Miss Gloria McKnight and her necklace of perfect attendance pins from Sunday school happened to sit nearby, we would suffer through paroxysms of laughter. We bit through the thumbs of several pairs of white cotton gloves as we tried to stem the giggles that always seemed to be waiting in the wings during the service.

We knew where the secret stairwell to the bell tower was and schemed about pulling the bell rope some day during the service. We loved the soaring beauty of the massive Gothic chancel where we sang. But we never actually discussed religion or what it meant to us.

In high school I went through a period of wondering about the Presbyterian belief in predestination. I had been agonizing over what would become of my life, but then realized maybe I shouldn't bother. God had a plan—which was at once comforting and bedeviling. Comforting in that it relieved me of having to be responsible for my life. Bedeviling in that I had trouble believing God actually knew my name and address.

We'd learned nothing about shotgun weddings as we grew up, except that they were not approved of and fodder for gossip for people like Miss McKnight. Sex was for after you were married, not before. Tucker's "situation" inspired a stern warning from my mother one afternoon.

"Don't you go pulling a trick like Tuck," she said as we waited for David Runkel, my fiancé, to arrive for the weekend.

"Mother, getting pregnant isn't exactly a trick. I'm not planning on getting pregnant for a very long time, and please don't talk to me that way."

"Well, it's easy to understand why Tucker's parents are upset—pregnant and the boy's *Catholic*," she said. "Don't take any chances is all I'm saying."

"Mother! Stop it. Tucker didn't mean to get pregnant. At least you don't have to worry about my becoming a Catholic, since David's family have been Pennsylvania Presbyterians for as long as our family has. And I don't really care if Tucker's pregnant or marrying a Catholic. We've been together since we were seven, and we'll be together until we're ninety-seven."

After that brief rehearsal, our Wednesday wedding got underway. The ceremony was stunning not just for its brevity but also for the intensity that emanated from the bride and groom. I saw him put his hand on her hip and couldn't help but feel aroused by his obvious knowledge of it. Tucker's romantic experience had definitely outdistanced my own. But I had reason to hope. Just the weekend before, David Runkel had asked me to marry him. *Finally*, the next wedding I'd attend would be my own.

On Palm Sunday, 1968, David and I were eager to get to church. By that time we were comfortably married and living in Baltimore. But Baltimore was on fire. Riots had erupted all over the city in response to the assassination of Martin Luther King, Jr. National Guardsmen carrying weapons with bayonets patrolled our block, sometimes stopping in our front yard. The night before, tanks had rumbled up and down the street. The irony of it all clouded our sleep—that the man of peace who in life inspired us to live in the inner city, in death left us in this chaos.

Even before our early Sunday breakfast, the phone began to ring. Tucker was among the callers concerned about our safety.

"We're fine, we're safe," I assured her. "It *is* a little scary, with the military and the fires. We had a little smoke in the house last night. No one really knows what's going to happen next. We're looking forward to going to church today though. It will be nice to be with other people and remember Dr. King. And get this—Marshall and the other three-year-olds will be spreading palms all the way up the aisle. We never got to do such a thing at Wayne Presbyterian, did we?"

When we moved to Baltimore, David and I had joined Second Presbyterian Church. Though we'd never really felt connected there, we remained part of the congregation, maybe out of habit. But everyone else seemed far better off and far less liberal. No one we'd met lived in the inner city, as we did, or in a row house. Even with all that, we looked forward to church as a potential refuge on this sad Palm Sunday. I fantasized on the way there that maybe we would all sing "We Shall Overcome" in Dr. King's memory. Maybe I would catch the hand of the person standing next to me and they would do the same, and eventually we'd all be joined as one in the face of this tragedy.

After the children's procession, we waited for a prayer for Dr. King. Then we waited for some reassuring scripture. We waited for a chance for the whole congregation to join together in acknowledging the gift of Dr. King's life. Just before the final benediction came the only acknowledgment of what had happened to our nation and our city: "The youth groups will not be meeting tonight due to the curfew."

We drove home feeling empty. The vague sense we'd had about Second Presbyterian had changed to concrete evidence. We didn't belong. David and I talked about the things we might have said about Martin Luther King during the service. David said even he could have offered an appropriate prayer. If he felt capable, why didn't the minister? In the process of giving ourselves the succor we'd been seeking at the church that day, we began to discover our own inner resources.

"We are writing to resign our membership in Second Presbyterian Church," our letter began. On the first page, it detailed our disappointment on Palm Sunday and then laid out our Presbyterian heredity: More than one branch of my own family had been called to this country from Scotland as Presbyterian ministers; David's family had been Presbyterians for more than 200 years. This was not a decision lightly taken we said, in words that made me cry every time I read them. "We understand now that authority for how we worship rests with us," we concluded.

I called Tucker the next day and read her the letter.

"Oh, Deed . . . . you must have felt like I did with the priest and the Catholic instruction. You didn't belong, right?" By this time, Tucker had divorced her husband on grounds of infidelity and taken the children out of the Catholic Sunday School she'd dutifully sent them to during her marriage.

"But can you believe it?" I said, still incredulous. "How could they not acknowledge Dr. Martin Luther King?"

"I'm not sure our parents and the Wayne Presbyterian Church would have either," Tucker said. "We'll just have to find a different church. Some of my friends here are Unitarians. I'm going to try that, even if I am an atheist."

"David and I will probably end up Quakers," I said. "We already go to anti-war and civil rights meetings at the American Friends Service Committee around the corner. Whatever we do, we've burned our bridge to the Presbyterian church, that's for sure."

At the Unitarian Church, Tucker found spiritual sustenance *and* a new husband. An atheist Unitarian like her, Jack became her wonderful, loving, brilliant husband. As they traveled the world, Tucker regularly sent me boxes for my collection. A small red apple from Manhattan, a beautiful round paper box from Florence, an enameled wooden oval box from Turkey. Tucker had an inimitable knack for picking out boxes she was sure I'd never get otherwise. "Unique like us," she'd say.

Not long after David and I sent our letter of resignation, we heard back from Second Presbyterian that it would be impossible to remove our names from the rolls. There were only two ways this could be accomplished: One, if we died. Two, if we became Catholics. Neither held much attraction. We thought of protesting what seemed to be an arcane rule but in the end decided to leave it alone.

⟳

Having been told I was unable to get pregnant again, David and I decided to adopt. We learned the process would be speedier if we chose a biracial child, which we were happy to do. However, one of the agency's requirements was proof that we had a relationship with a religious organization. *Should we quickly look for a new church? But how much time would that take?* Neither dead nor Catholic, we knew our names were still on the rolls at Second Presbyterian . . .

With fear and trepidation, I placed the call and was informed that a temporary pastor was now in charge.

"We'd like to invite the minister to our house," I said as warmly as I could, explaining the adoption proceedings.

"I'm sure he'd enjoy meeting you," the secretary said. *She must be new too.* "He's originally from Florida and is just getting used to the North."

Oh my God! He's from Florida. He's probably opposed to interracial adoptions, and we'll end up never getting our baby. I was panic-stricken, but what else could we do?

The night of the minister's visit, David and I were very nervous. *He must have read our letter of resignation. He'll probably be uncomfortable in our neighborhood.* Marsh was in bed, and I had put cookies in the oven to make our guest feel welcome. When the doorbell rang, we both jumped a few feet.

As it turned out, the visiting minister had read our letter and said he wanted to begin by acknowledging our disappointments and congratulating us on our heartfelt expectations. He said he'd only been at the church a short while, but he could already see how uncomfortable and unsupported we must have felt there. He said our desires for equality and civil rights had a strong Christian base, and he was in total support of them. "There are just two things I want to ask you to do in preparation for getting this lucky baby," he said.

The timer went off in the kitchen. I excused myself and returned a few minutes later with a plate of warm cookies, incredulous at the direction of our talk.

"Would you like something to drink?" I asked.

"No, Deedie. No need to make a fuss. I just want to leave some homework for you two. I think you both could benefit from reading Paul's letters to the Corinthians," he said. Our jaws dropped. "As you may know, Paul had a lot to say. He was full of fear and didn't feel welcome on the island of Corinth. He saw divisions in the church and didn't know how to heal them. I think Paul may help heal what I can see has been a bruising experience for you.

"And the second thing I would ask is that you bring your baby to the church. Not for baptism, unless you want to. Just to be acknowledged. I think your baby might have the power to teach this church a great deal. Please stay in touch with me in the coming months, and let me know if I can help."

David and I were sitting on the sofa. I moved closer to him. The minister leaned toward us and smiled warmly, then got up and took another cookie.

Stunned, nearly speechless, David and I got up to shake his hand. He gave me a hug instead. As we closed the door behind him, the part of Paul's letters I did know, having heard it at nearly every wedding I'd been in, came to mind: "And now these three remain—faith, hope and love, and the greatest of these is love."

❦

The first Sunday we ever went to Quaker meeting, I felt like I'd returned home.

I remember walking from my office in Philadelphia to the Meeting House, wondering if my Beeson ancestors, who were Quakers, had walked the same street. In the silence of the meeting, I became familiar with what was inside me for the first time. I learned to bypass the clamor of what I *should* do to discern what I *could* do. My soul now had its own community, and inside myself I had a reliable source of inspiration.

More than a year into our life as Quakers, one Sunday, deep into meditation, my heart began to beat faster. My cheeks reddened. I straightened up, not totally sure what was happening. I listened. What had been a theme for my meditation had become a full thought—a message. How could I be sure? I waited a little longer. My heartbeat began to accelerate. I put both hands on the bench in front of me to steady myself and realized I was pulling myself into a standing position. David and the children looked up in shock. My hands and legs were shaking.

"I am experiencing the full meaning of ministry today. I see that it is an obligation we have to each other. It is not something that is done to us or given to us. It comes from us to others and from others to us."

I sat down. My heart was returning to its normal beat, but I was still shaking. David took my hand in his. Marshall's twelve-year-old rough hand came down on the other. We belonged to each other and to the Meeting.

⊗

One day Tucker called to say I would be receiving documents from the Diocese of Harrisburg—a petition for annulment filed by her former husband. As a Catholic, he couldn't marry the woman with whom he'd been living unless his fifteen-year marriage to Tucker was declared null. Twenty-five years later! Annulled! By whose authority? As a witness to the wedding, I was being asked by the Tribunal of the Diocese to comment on whether the couple had been faithful, used birth control, or ever talked about divorce before they were married. Apparently an affirmative answer to the latter two would provide the basis for a successful annulment. Was this supposed to erase the fact that they had actually been married, that they'd had two children and spent fifteen years as husband and wife? Wouldn't their children be illegitimate if we pretended the marriage never existed? I returned the sixteen-page document with "Unanswerable" written in most of the blanks.

Tucker and I still laugh about the Catholic church requesting testimony from a Quaker and a Unitarian. We never did find out what happened with the annulment. But one day on the phone the Presbyterian Sunday School girls got the giggles again.

"Well, Tuck, for all we know," I said, "the outcome of the Tribunal was probably predestined."

Peels of laughter lifted our hearts as we recognized how far we had come together and how delighted we were to have made the "greatest" choice—to live out the days of our lives in love.

CHAPTER EIGHT

Peace Prize

"You all know who this is, don't you?"

"Marshall's Mom!" thirty ten-year-olds say in unison. Then louder, in chaos: "Marshall's Mom!" "Hi, Miss Rumpel." "Hi, Marshall's mom. I know *you*."

Samuel J. Lester, the principal of Steele Elementary School, had urgently but gently pushed me through the doorway of the fifth-grade class room. If Career Day was to have any meaning for Miss Sweet's class, he'd needed to come up with a quick replacement for a speaker who'd dropped out. I was his handy, albeit unprepared, recruit.

Although David and I were the organizers of this event, I'd appointed myself as a troubleshooter rather than a speaker. I hadn't been able to imagine how I would ever explain to elementary school kids my job as Community Relations Specialist. Now that I'd been so abruptly recruited, what was I going to say? Panic seized me. But as I listened to those voices greeting me in recognition of what to them was my most important role, inspiration struck.

"Today we're going to talk about what it takes to be a mom," I began. "You all know that I'm Marshall's mom, and you also know something else. What does any mom need to know how to do? Will you help me make a list of what skills are required for the job? Then, after we look at the list together, we'll decide what kind of training is necessary. Okay? Let's get started."

Hands shot up, and it wasn't long before the blackboard was full of what these children knew it took to be a mom. She has to be: good at math, a negotiator, a nurse, good at dressing up, sympathetic, able to write letters and read, know how to drive, have lots of recipes and know how to cook, know the best places to shop and how to sew, be able to sing songs, full of love but strict when she has to be . . . The list went on and on. One girl appeared to be disappointed I hadn't called on her for her second suggestion, so I asked her what it was.

"She has to believe in God. That's important," she said.

By the end of the hour, I'd come to appreciate the enormity of my job as a mom, my *career* as a mom, to a far greater degree than ever before.

It was the 1970s, and I was busy being an early role model not just for Mom, but for Super Mom. I had miraculously (so it seemed to me) had a second child, a little sister for Marshall. But I soon discovered that spending all day with two young children and housework made me feel trapped and overwhelmed. I'd lose my temper with Marshall over minor issues and bathe in guilt over it for days. Maybe we needed a break from each other.

I found a nearly fulltime job as a Community Relations agent for the first school district in the North to undergo court-ordered desegregation. I considered myself very fortunate to be combining my avocation of doing good in the community with my vocation of public relations. I got to write a lot. Talk to reporters. Go to school board meetings. It was fulfilling, which I know made me a better mom at home.

I seemed to be succeeding at *both* my careers. Marshall was excelling at school, and he qualified for lots of benefits, including the Gifted and Talented program. As a fifth grader in 1976, he spent so much time studying Pennsylvania history in independent study that when the National Governors' Conference came to town, he was tapped to head up the Children's Program. I was full of pride that he was teaching other kids about the battles at Gettysburg and the Declaration of Independence.

However, a week or so after Career Day at his school, I had a wake-up call. We were on our way to the grocery store, Marshall and a friend of his in the back seat of the car, and I was eavesdropping. What I heard took Super Mom down a notch.

"Hey, man, you gotta stop giving up your lunch money and just fight once," Cody said to Marshall.

"I'm not a fighter," Marsh replied. In the rearview mirror, I could see him folding his arms across his chest, puffing it out a little.

"They're gonna keep hittin you up 'til you fight, man," Cody counseled.

"It's not worth it to me. I'd rather go without lunch."

I turned down the radio so I could hear better. *What? Marsh's lunch money is being hijacked everyday? Why wasn't I aware of this?*

"Marsh, what's Cody talking about? Is there a problem at school?" I tried not to sound as alarmed as I was.

"Mom, it's nothing. Cody's just spouting off," he said, elbowing Cody in the side.

"So, what did you have for lunch today?" I asked.

"Do you remember, Cody? I can't," Marsh said.

"You better tell your Ma the truth," I heard Cody say under his breath.

When David got home, I told him we had a problem. "Deedie, this is just one of those kid things. I'll talk to him about fighting. He has to learn about it some day," David responded. "It just isn't a big deal."

I was in pain. Here I thought I had my finger on the pulse of Marshall's life, and I didn't. I hadn't even been paying attention when, a few weeks earlier, our housekeeper had asked if it was all right for her to give the kids an early dinner at five because Marsh was so hungry every day. I promised myself I'd pay more attention to the details of his daily life, and cried as I went to sleep.

At the end of that school year, David's newspaper transferred him to Philadelphia, so after five years in Harrisburg, we moved. Marsh no longer worried about lunch-money heists because lunch was included in the cost of tuition at Friends Central, a private Quaker school.

As he had in Harrisburg, Marsh, accompanied by our Dalmation Leonard Cohen, delivered the newspaper each day before school, becoming in the process the best friend of every elderly lady in the apartment building next door to us. For the first time, he had a bunch of neighborhood boys as friends, and our turn-of-the-century huge grey stone house, with a wrap-around front porch and finished basement, became their headquarters.

At Friends Central, Marsh blossomed into a boy who was as much at ease on the football field as he was playing the bouncer in "Cabaret." But for us, it was a financial sea change. Working was no longer something I did for my mental health, it was a necessity. And we ate pasta a lot more frequently than we ever had before.

I would work hard all day then set out for home to work at my hardest job. Decompressing on the train, I'd plan dinner and try to remember who had what activity that evening. I'd read the newspaper and arrive at my stop relatively relaxed. But somehow, in the short walk up to the house, my sense of peace would disappear. I'd walk through the front door and blow my fuse.

"How can you say you respect me but leave the kitchen in such a mess every afternoon?" I wasn't shouting, I was screaming at the top of my lungs, and it was happening a lot.

"Mom, it's not such a big deal. We'll take care of it," Marsh would say, rallying the help of whichever friends were cowering in the basement. "Did you have a bad day at the office or something?"

If I wasn't screaming at him for not practicing the piano, cleaning his room, washing the dishes, or doing his homework, it was for not collecting his newspaper money or for picking on his sister. Sometimes I'd lie awake at night, my throat sore from having screamed so much.

I don't know exactly what fueled those explosions. Was it driven by my constant guilt that I was working and so not giving my children proper oversight? Perhaps I was suffering the downside of being Super Mom. Whatever it was, I simply couldn't figure out a different way to do it, a different way to be a mother.

Three years later, when David was offered a transfer to Washington, DC, Marsh announced he wasn't going to enroll in school there.

"Sidwell Friends School is not only the best school in Washington, it's one of the best in the country," I said, shocked at this unexpected idea. "Why wouldn't you go there?"

"I just think I'd be happier at Westtown. It has everything I want, and Philadelphia's where I belong," he said. I couldn't help thinking that my six foot-four-inch boy whom I still considered little, wanted to go away to escape my own bad parenting.

Wanting to respect his initiative but thinking it would feel unnatural not to have him with us for high school, David and I countered with what we were sure would be insurmountable obstacles.

"Marsh, if you are really, really serious about going to Westtown, here are the conditions under which we'll consider it: One, you complete all the requirements for the application yourself—tests, recommendations, essays. Two, apply for a scholarship that would make up the difference between Sidwell's tuition and Westtown's. Okay?"

"That's great, Mom and Dad, I can do that," he said enthusiastically.

I was skeptical. For all of his talents and accomplishments, organizing himself to brush his teeth every day was still a challenge.

On his own steam, Marsh got accepted to both Westtown and Sidwell. He chose Westtown. I knew I'd failed as a mom. The evidence was clear. No wonder he wanted to get away. All that screaming. Anyone would. I'd *driven* him away. When our friends wanted to know why Marsh was in boarding school, all I could say was it was his choice because he was so unhappy in Washington. The only thing that gave me comfort was the fact he would be going to a fine school, one of the oldest in the country. But for months every Saturday morning, I'd sit in the kitchen expecting him to come up to breakfast any minute. And then I'd recall how it was my fault he wasn't there.

Marshall flourished for most of the first year, both as a student and a leader in the community. I marveled at how correct he was in knowing what was best for himself. How great to be so self-possessed at such an early age.

But along with a wonderful bunch of new friends came pot. Pete, Toby, Sam, Hunter . . . . all of them bright and talented, apparently spent a great deal of time smoking, perched on slate roofs first installed in 1799. Each time they were caught, another opportunity was lost. For Marsh, his chances for being president of the student body ended. By his senior year, even though he was a National Merit semi-finalist, his grades were only so-so, foreclosing on the possibility of getting into a top-ranked college.

I couldn't yell at him long distance, but I wanted to. I thought back to the list of things moms had to know in order to be a good parent. "Teach your kid to make good choices," I'd written on the blackboard. I'd flunked that one, for sure. Where had we gone wrong? Where was he headed? Didn't he care about what became of him? Whenever we brought up his dope-smoking, he'd become belligerent and say it was no more harmful than the glass of wine we had with dinner. I couldn't help but think that Marsh was as disappointed as we were, but that wasn't the conversation we were having.

Home briefly before he left for Earlham College, Marshall went with us to Bethesda Friends Meeting one Sunday. I'd been trying hard to focus on all of his positive potential, not always successfully. To my astonishment, that day Marsh rose to speak, for the first time. *What was he going to say? What was he thinking?* I was nervous, afraid we'd all be embarrassed.

In a strong, powerful voice, his message came. "When we lived in Philadelphia, I delivered papers every morning at six. Every day without fail, I'd see the mother of my best friends on her way to Mass. I'd been to Mass before, because her sons signed me up as an altar boy before they knew I wasn't Catholic. But I was always amazed that Monica could leave their apartment every morning and go off to church. What did she find there, I always wondered.

"Today as I think about it again, I am grateful for her example. Without realizing it, she taught me the importance of faith, and that's very important, isn't it? You have to have faith, especially in yourself."

He sat down. I was shaking. He was shaking. Our bench was almost shaking. David put his hand on Marsh's. I felt relieved—and proud. On our way out, someone told me how moving Marsh's words had been. She knew I'd been concerned about him and said she hoped his words had helped restore *my* faith in him. Maybe they had, but I also wished I had been as good an example for him as Monica had been.

Five years later, Marsh had given college a try, traveled and lived overseas and was now working fulltime as a tree planter. While I certainly believed it was important to plant trees, this somehow did not match the professional trajectory I'd imagined for him. I'd begun to despair that he had lost his faith in himself. That Christmas he arrived in Belize, where David and I were working, and was an instant sensation among the young women in my office. Tall and handsome, he had a thick dark brown braid down the middle of his back and a ruggedness about him that exuded strength and goodwill.

"Mom, I've decided one of your Christmas presents is going to be a haircut.

What do you think? Isn't it about time I got rid of the hippy look? I'm going back to college soon. A new look, a new beginning," he said, settling his long body into a chair in my office.

"Bean," I said, using my favorite nickname for this long, skinny son of mine, "Your hair really doesn't bother me anymore. It actually looks pretty good. But if you need a recommendation for a barber, go talk to Katherine and Stephanie. They'll know where you should go, who should do it. Don't do it just for me, though, really. And be sure to save it."

As I left work that day, I asked the staff where they'd sent Marsh for his haircut.

"Oh, we wouldn't let him do it, Miss Deedie. Beautiful hair like that? It would have been a crime. Are you upset? Did you want that braid gone?"

When I got home, David and Marsh were having a drink. His braid was intact.

"I couldn't do it, Mom. Those girls wouldn't let me," he said, getting up to give me a hug and kiss.

My Christmas present instead was a book *I, Rigoberta*, by Rigoberta Menchú, an indigenous Guatemalan who became a spokesperson for her people. She'd won the Nobel Peace Prize that year. Marshall watched eagerly as I opened to the inscription. Tears came to my eyes as I read: *Mom, You deserve to have won many a peace prize for your work in our family. Rigoberta's story sounded uncannily familiar to me, having grown up with such a powerful person as my mother. Thank you for helping me to discover what a terrible and terrific world surrounds us. As I grow, I have begun to realize and appreciate . . . . lessons less taught than assimilated . . .* I could barely read on through the tears. Here sat the boy I'd spent so much of my voice yelling at. Yet through it all, he'd heard what I was about. He'd known that I was better, perhaps, than I did. I hugged him until we both sat down and cried.

⸙

"Mom. I almost forgot." Marsh stopped us on our way out the door. "I've been looking and looking for a box for your collection. I didn't find one, but Mel did, with Ramona's help." By this time, Marshall was married to Melissa and was the father of three-year-old Ramona. "What do you think?" He took a small silver box off the mantel and placed it in my hand.

We were visiting them in Portland, where Marsh was starting up a "green" business and involved in local politics. He'd worked as an assistant to a City Hall Commissioner, and Mel told me one of the reasons she fell in love with him was that they could barely get down the street without someone coming up to thank him for something he'd done. This boy had done me proud.

I looked down to see what he had given me, and there was a silver filigreed box. Embedded in the lid was a ceramic tile with a blue and white image of a peacock, its tail feathers unfurled. All the way back home I held it in my hand, cherishing how proud we are of each other.

CHAPTER NINE

Unexpected Light

"Listen to this, Lucy! Listen."

We were in the car, and NPR was doing one of its reports from the *New England Journal of Medicine*. This one documented the fact that the personalities of infants who have had to fight for their lives at birth are often prickly, maybe a little vinegary. Many have trust issues based on the rough treatment they may have gotten in the rush to save their lives. They have a tendency to be loners because they had to be their own champion fresh from the womb.

David and I were spellbound. They were talking about our daughter, the one in the back seat. They could have been reading from her medical records. Cord around the neck. Not enough air. Hole in her lung. Emergency surgery. Neo-natal intensive care for a week. They were talking about this person whom we sometimes couldn't believe was our daughter, she was so outspoken and pissant.

Lucy was fifteen and at that moment wearing an orange blouse, Liz Claiborne orange plaid skirt from my sister, and orange socks her Grandmother bought her. The reason I still know what color she was wearing is that she wore orange every day for the entire year she was fifteen. Her efforts to be orange-clad were supported by everyone who knew and loved her. Orange articles of clothing, not easy to find in those days, arrived in the mail regularly.

"So Lucy, did you hear? What do you think? Isn't that amazing? Don't you find it fascinating?" I was sputtering, I was so excited to hear someone explain why one of the persons dearest to me on earth could also be so ornery.

"Bullshit, mom. That's all bullshit and you know it. How could they ever prove something like that?"

I looked over at David, who was smiling. "Case rests, I guess," he muttered for just me to hear. I started to laugh.

"What are you laughing about? What's so funny about it, even if it does happen to be true?" She draped her long arms over the back of both our seats.

"It's just funny that you think it's all bullshit, that's all. I've heard the theory before, but never this thoroughly. I waded in a little further. "You know, Lucy, even if there's even a shred of truth to it, it could explain why you sometimes feel really bad about how other people treat you."

"Yes," David added, "And I've always thought there's a chance that maybe there wasn't enough anesthesia used when they opened your chest, and if so, you must have experienced excruciating pain. That could make you maybe not trust people."

"Especially us, since we're your parents and we're responsible," I said, my eyes filling up with unexpected tears.

"Can we stop at McDonald's so I can get some McNuggets?" Lucy responded.

Lucy's dramatic entry into our lives was the culminating scene of what had felt like a mystery-adventure-and-love story, all rolled into one. Seven months before her birth, David and

I had been busily preparing for the arrival of an adopted baby. One morning when I was working on what would be the nursery, David stopped in to kiss me good-bye. "You're getting really chesty," he said, and gave me a feel as he left.

I was standing next to the closet. David never said anything about how I looked. And a feel! In the morning! What was different today? I turned and looked in the mirror. I didn't look "chesty" to myself. I took off my sweater and looked again. No. My bra seemed to be the right size, but when I put my hands under my breasts, I realized there was more there than usual, and maybe they were a little tender. Could I be *pregnant*? How could that be? When did I have a period? No, that didn't really count with me. I was always having periods or not having them at all because of the endometriosis. Maybe I *was* pregnant.

What would we do? How could we have two babies at once? Well, we could do it. We'd make it work. One thought after another tumbled in a perfect frenzy as my mind tackled the notion. I looked around the nursery, where a friend had begun painting Beatrix Potter figures on the wall. *Could there be two cribs? I'd better get to work. No, I'd better find out if I really was pregnant first.* Two of the world's best fertility doctors had told me there was no chance at all of my ever getting pregnant again. And they'd reiterated this to our social worker at the adoption agency. Within a few minutes, I was saying words I never thought I'd hear myself say again.

"This is Donnan Runkel. I'm calling Dr. Georgeanna Jones to inform her I might be pregnant." The secretary said she'd check with Dr. Jones and call me back.

Minutes later, the phone rang. "I checked with the doctor and she says she doesn't think it's possible, but you should wait a month to see if you have a period and then call."

I couldn't wait a month to find out. I was feeling more pregnant with every gathering moment. I decided to go directly to Johns Hopkins to Dr. Jones's office to see if I could convince her in person to run a pregnancy test *now*. I found a jelly jar in the pantry and peed into it.

When I got home, I called the social worker at the adoption agency to tell her I might be pregnant. She said they'd have to put the brakes on our getting a baby until we knew. We couldn't adopt a baby if I was pregnant. I was crushed. Marshall would soon be five and we still didn't have the second child we'd wanted so badly for years. All of our friends already had two children.

The pregnancy was confirmed the next day. When I asked Dr. Georgeanna how someone with only a speck of an ovary could now be pregnant—and nearly three months at that—she said, "This baby is quite determined to be born, that's all I can tell you. The odds against it were overwhelming. This is going to be a very special baby."

❧

For the first few months after Lucy's traumatic arrival, I spent hours watching over her, rocking her, feeding her even if she hadn't asked to be fed. One day a friend came to visit and found me in the nursery, a pile of magazines, books and newspapers around my feet. A dachshund named Hans and a sleeping infant shared my lap. "Deedie, you can't spend *all* your time up here," she said.

"I have to. What if something happens to her breathing? I just couldn't stand it if I wasn't here to help," I said.

"But don't you remember the doctor telling you this was going to be a remarkable child? She wanted to be born so badly you got pregnant when no one thought you could? I think you should consider yourself on safe ground now that she's here and healthy. Look how big she is."

I stroked Lucy's silky little head and looked up. "You're right. But it's really hard not to be afraid. Really hard," I said.

Before we knew it, that tiny head had become the repository for a vast storehouse of knowledge and information. Lucy spent hours reading every book the library would lend her. Everyone gave her books for presents. When she discovered a new topic, her quest became feverish. Her interest in mythology began with the ancient Greeks when she was nine but soon stretched to include Norse and Roman tales.

"I'm a mythologist," she told people matter-of-factly. No one bothered to ask her what a mythologist did. And when she was asked what she wanted to be when she grew up, it was "an Egyptologist."

How could this little girl's brain know and retain so much more than mine when I was four times older than she was? *I* could never remember why Demeter was important, but Lucy could, as well as who this particular goddess was related to and where she spent her time in Greece. I quickly realized that the important thing as Lucy's parent was to make sure she always had books. If she had a book to read and a back-up, she was secure.

But adolescence posed a challenge to this person whose life depended on the turning of a page. The unwritten laws of social integration and cliquedom proved exceptionally challenging; the rules were not to be found in a book and friends couldn't be checked out at the library. The other Quaker girls at Sidwell Friends School could be counted on for support, but then there were others like Ariel Boscom. She was the epitome of all Lucy disliked about Sidwell.

"I *hate* Ariel Boscom. She's just so mean and superior. And she acts like she knows everything. Why is she so popular?" Lucy wailed one night.

"What did Ariel do to you?" I asked.

"Oh, she's just mean about me wearing orange. Says I'm trying to get attention by doing it."

"Well, why *are* you wearing orange every day?" I asked, hoping there might be a new answer. Maybe something based on an ancient rite she'd read about of young women entering their sixteenth years wearing orange to help shift their own self image from someone under the influence of parents to someone who was self-possessed. Maybe it was a ritual of self-love dictated by Diana, the goddess of love. *Please, Lucy*, I remember thinking, *please think of something good*.

"Mom, get off my case! I'm wearing orange every day because I want to, and besides, it's better than black like everyone else wears. Why do you wear pantyhose every day to the office? Is it because you want to?"

"Well, I was just thinking that you might be able to satisfy Ariel if you came up with a really clever reason why you're wearing orange."

"It's really none of your business or Ariel's, Mom."

"I was only trying to help, Lucy."

"I have homework." And off she went. I slumped onto the table. I just didn't know how to be present to this child, who was clearly having many of the same issues I'd had navigating high school. I couldn't seem to reach her heart and give it the first aid I thought it needed. Why was this so hard for me? For her? Was it the school? I sometimes didn't feel any more comfortable there than she did, but where else could she get the great education she was getting? Was it her early trauma? Could that really be it?

At the end of her second year at the University of Chicago, to which she'd been steered by her counselor at Sidwell, Lucy announced she was going to take some time off. Maybe she'd work. Maybe she'd travel. Maybe she'd just think for a while. She was hoping to have access to the money we would have spent on tuition.

"The money's for tuition, Lucy, not for freestyle spending," I said. "Don't you think it would be a better idea to just finish up and then do some relaxing and exploring? You've been so happy there and have so many friends."

"Well then I'll just spend my own money," she countered. "Rachel and I are going on a trip around the country. It'll take us most of the year."

Once they were on the road, we received fairly regular updates by phone. Here we are in East Jesus, Mississippi. Here we are in Athens, Georgia. Did you know Texas was so huge and there are Quakers here too? Do we know anyone in Santa Fe? We're going to Pasadena from there.

One day when I was at work, an urgent call came through from Lucy. Calling at the office was only for emergencies.

"Have you been in a crash?" I asked right away.

"No, Mom. We're fine. I just have to know if I've gotten any mail from the Dean at the University."

"No, there hasn't been anything. What would the Dean be writing you about?"

"Oh, I decided to apply for re-admission next semester. We're going to speed this trip up because we're running out of money."

"Well, I really can't help you with this one, Lucy. If you want to reach the Dean, I think you're going to have to do the reaching. You took a year's leave of absence. I don't really know how these things work, but I think you're pushing it." I felt irritated, but maybe a little delighted at the same time that she was getting back to academics. "But I thought this call was a crisis since you were calling at the office."

"Mom, I'm not asking you to handle it. I just wanted to know if the mail had anything for me. I wrote the Dean a poem asking for re-admission."

"You wrote the Dean of the University of Chicago a *poem* asking for re-admission?" I shot back. "Lucy, that's no way to do business. Honestly, I can't believe you. The world is not sitting around waiting for you to write poems about your intentions, even if they're good ones."

"Cool your jets, Mom. You don't have to do anything. I'm sorry for calling at work. I'll check in a few days to see if anything's come yet. Then I may call Chicago. Don't you think that's a good plan?"

"Lucy, I have no idea. I just don't think you should count on being back in school in January. This is December, you know."

Several days later, I tore open the letter from Chicago and read it, stunned. The Dean had written back, re-admitting her, in verse. It read in part:

> How could we resist this chance,
>
> To have a student back whose life enhances . . .

"See, Mom. It pays to be creative, right?" Lucy said that night when she called.

"You're always saying that, right?"

"Yup. That. *Is.* What. *I'm.* Al*ways.* Say*ing.* My *dear,*" I replied in iambic pentameter.

This emerging young woman had finally awakened me to the realization that she was quite literally in the driver's seat. It didn't matter what had happened in the very beginning to threaten her life, nor how sentimental I felt about getting pregnant in the first place. It didn't matter at all that I'd named her Lucy, just like my mother and grandmother and me, and that it meant light. And it didn't even matter that she came to us unexpectedly in December at Christmas time and lay in a basket under the tree. These were incidental to a life she was creating that was now totally her own.

After Peace Corps in Yemen, where she learned Arabic, her third language, Lucy returned to Chicago to continue teaching English as a Second Language. I was on hand for one of the graduation ceremonies for her students. In the cavernous basement of St. Stanislaus Roman Catholic Church in the center of Hyde Park, twenty-three of Ms. Runkel's students were set to get their certificates. Their families were on hand to witness the event, and food from their countries of origin was heating up in the kitchen. Even the dim lighting couldn't dampen their high spirits.

I watched Ms. Runkel take the stage. As if she belonged to someone else, I was struck by this tall, slim beauty with blue eyes full of light, dark hair falling in curls around her face.

"This is a special day for all of us," Lucy said as she opened the ceremony. "We want to recognize each of you for your hard work toward learning to speak and write English. And I also want to introduce you to the person who taught me so much of what I know—my mom, Deedie Runkel. She has helped make sure lots and lots of people all over the world get access to education, but especially me. You wouldn't believe all she did to make sure I would be standing in front of you today. Since most of you are also moms, you should meet her. She's the best."

Tears spilled from my eyes as each of the students seated near me turned to give a nod or a wink. The woman next to me squeezed my arm.

After each had received a certificate to much clapping and cheering, Maris from Lithuania and Teresa from Mexico went to the front of the room with their own presentation for their teacher.

"We want to thank you, Lucy, for all your patience," Maris said slowly and distinctly.

"And your love," Teresa interrupted, smiling broadly and nodding vigorously.

"We want to wish you good luck in the future, wherever you are, even it's in Chile," Maris continued, acknowledging Lucy's announcement that that was her next destination. She handed Lucy a card and a package.

Lucy's eyes had tears in them as she opened the card and began to read it aloud for the group. "We're so sorry at your loss," it began.

Lucy looked up at me with a little smile and went on reading. The sympathy card her students had found for her perfectly expressed the sorrow they felt at losing her.

⸮

Christmas is always a big deal at our house. Even in a year when we agree we're going to be modest, there's too much. One year after hours of exchanging gifts, Lucy appeared at my side and sat down on the arm of the chair.

"I forgot your biggest present, Mama."

"Whatever could it be? There's so much already," I said.

Lucy slumped all the way into my lap, all six feet of her, and put a tiny package in my hand. I wrapped my arms around her and holding the present in front of both of us, I opened it.

"Did you get another box for your collection?" David asked, coming into the room with more coffee.

"Yup, she did," Lucy said smugly.

I lifted out a small royal blue ceramic box about the size of a very small tangerine. The large orangey flower on the top has yellow, blue and purple leaves. The lid fit perfectly.

Lucy took it from me. "Look at this, Mama." She turned it upside down. "The artist's name is Nuri. That means "light" in Arabic."

CHAPTER TEN

The Gift

"See, here are your three children," the palmist said confidently. She was pointing to the three creases at the base of my extended little finger.

"Well, I'm afraid you're wrong there. I have two children, and I'm quite certain I won't be having another. I've had a hysterectomy. It's just not possible," I said. *She must be a quack. What will David say when he finds out I've spent $60 we don't have to get this little nugget of information?*

That I'd resorted to a palm reader for direction was a sign of just how desperate I was. The newspaper where David had been a reporter had closed, and he was unhappy in his new job. I was still smarting from Marshall's decision to go to boarding school in Pennsylvania instead of spending his high school years at home with us. My own job at the time was rallying mainstream women to convince their elected officials that the world's stash of nuclear weapons threatened our security rather than safeguarded it. The fact that we woke up every morning and there hadn't been a nuclear war wasn't producing enough job satisfaction for me. Now here I was hoping my palm might reveal a new direction for my life.

The palmist wasn't wearing a turban like they do at the circus, but her untamed long, curly red hair and green eyes lent an exotic air. I couldn't help noticing that everything visible in the room was in a different shade of green. And we were sitting at a table covered with a shiny, slimy-olive-green cloth.

She continued with her explication of what my hands revealed about my life thus far, and what they portended for my future.

"You've had some difficult roads to travel, Mrs. Runkel, that's clear. Being the youngest child is never easy. *How did she know that?* And you've had a few very scary health issues, haven't you?" she asked, looking up from my hand while pointing to the evidence. "What I can't get over is what a strong spirit you have. That's what's gotten you through." Smiling directly at me, she went on, "I'm sure people like to work with you." *That could be said about almost anyone.*

"Life is particularly challenging for people like yourself. You take on big jobs, and feel intense responsibility for making sure everything goes right for everyone else. The trick is to determine what *you* really want to do and go toward that. Otherwise, you'll always feel as if you're stuck fulfilling other people's goals. It's all right here in this hand," she said, tapping the middle of my right palm with her left index finger. The nails were painted pale green.

❦

Less than a year later, we were having the rare family dinner with everyone present. Marshall was home for Spring Break, and I'd prepared all the food he said he'd missed—lamb, roasted potatoes, asparagus. The phone rang and David got up to answer it. The children and I continued talking—until we heard David's voice from the kitchen, an agonizing, "Oh no. No, no. Oh no."

Slowly, we each pushed back from the table, got up and made our way to him. Still on the phone, David wasn't saying anything, just shaking his head and pounding his fist lightly on the counter. I grabbed his hand, tried to hear what someone on the other end of the line was saying. Marsh put his arm around my shoulder. Lucy wiggled in next to her dad.

"I have very bad news from New Mexico," he said flatly after he hung up. "Susan and Mike are both dead. It's just . . . . it's just . . . . too horrible for words," he said, his chin sinking into his chest, his right arm reaching out to clutch Lucy's shoulder. Susan was David's little, and only, sister. Mike had put a violent end to both their lives. Sara, their daughter, was five years old. We stood, arms entwined, heads together. Lucy started crying.

After a few minutes Marsh broke away. "What do we need to do, Dad?" he asked in a strong voice. Without waiting for an answer, he picked up the phone. I couldn't imagine what he was doing, who he might be calling, but I was too shocked to do anything but cling to David and Lucy.

"Susie, it's Marshall. Something terrible's happened. Can you and Dan come right over?" he said, sounding very much in command. How did he know that the best thing to do would be to call our close friends?

❧

Just a few months earlier, we'd spent Thanksgiving together at the farm in northwestern Pennsylvania where David, his older brother Art, and Susan had grown up. Their mother, whom we all called Nana, was hosting us for the holiday. Susan, Mike and little Sara were there from New Mexico. Nana had interrupted the usual raucous round of storytelling to begin a discussion about wills. She wanted us all to know what was in hers. Widowed by that point for five years, she was taking charge of her future. Susan said she and Mike were doing their wills for the first time. She turned to David and me:

"If any thing happened to us, would it be okay for us to put the two of you down as guardians?" she asked.

"Really?" I said, a little taken aback.

"Yes, we were going to ask friends, but then we decided against it in favor of family," she said.

"Of course, we'd be honored," David said. I was quiet.

Any honor I felt was tarnished by guilt and jealousy. Guilt that I had somehow never mastered the skill of listening to my kids. Guilt that I screamed at them. And jealous that Susan seemed to have gotten it right, right from the beginning. She was the best mother I'd ever seen. She listened, she was patient, she didn't yell. That she would choose *me* was practically unfathomable.

After talking through the evening about the tragedy, we all finally retired. I couldn't get Thanksgiving off my mind. David and I were in bed but couldn't sleep.

"Do you think we're really going to get Sara?" I asked him, turning over to face him, my hand on his cheek. "I want to be as good a mother as Susan was."

"Don't worry, Deedie. *Please* don't worry," he said, squeezing my hand. "We have to try to sleep."

The next morning as we were waking up, Lucy and Marshall came in. I couldn't believe Marsh was awake at this hour. Lucy snuggled her gangly thirteen-year-old body down between us. We were all quiet.

"What will happen to Sara?" Lucy asked, starting to cry again.

"We don't know for absolutely sure," David said, putting his arms around her. "But you're probably going to end up with a little sister."

Later that day David and I were sitting next to each other when he turned and said with half a smile, "So, do you think you can be a mom all over again?"

I started to say something but instead found myself heaving with wrenching sobs, so powerful my jaw hurt. Tears ran over my cheeks and down my neck. I leaned my head back and felt a rush of tears run behind my ears into my hair. Every time I tried to say something, a huge hiccup of a sob would rumble up my raw throat. My hands were trembling. My legs were shaking.

After a few minutes, I managed to take a deep breath. My hands and legs quieted down. "I only hope I can do as well as Susan did." My voice was back.

"You'll do fine," David said, then quickly added, his voice breaking, "*We'll* do fine."

"I'm going to try to never scream again," I said. I was determined that, having suffered such a gigantic loss, Sara's life with us would be one of opportunity and happiness.

The first month after her parents' death, Sara remained on the farm with Nana. She had always loved visiting there with her mother, and now she was spending hours playing with Susan's old costumes from dancing school and the toys Nana had saved from Susan's childhood. But at sixty-seven, Nana felt she was too old to become a fulltime mom again, and she thought a family with other children would be best for Sara. We'd all agreed that at the end of that month, she and Sara would come to our home in Maryland, and we would tell Sara we were her new family.

After dinner one night, we all gathered in the living room on the two facing sofas. Sara was glued to Nana's side. Lucy chose to sit on Sara's other side. Marsh, home for the weekend, sat across from them between David and me.

David started. "Sara, we want to talk about a very big change for you. Nana's going to go back to the farm tomorrow, and you're going to stay here to live with us and be part of our family."

Lucy moved over closer, but Sara wrenched away from her and climbed into Nana's lap. "No, no I'm not," she screamed. She began crying uncontrollably. Nana rocked her back and forth, tears dripping down her face onto this offspring and last vestige of her dead daughter. We had all decided beforehand it would be good if we didn't cry, but it proved to be a very hard assignment. Lucy leaned over to stroke Sara's back, tears streaming down her cheeks.

Leaning across the coffee table, Marsh said, "Sara, listen to me. I'm your big brother now. There's an upside to this deal. You get a brother *and* a sister. We know how hard it must be for you, but we love you and want you to be in our family."

"Yeah, Sara. I've never had a little sister and I've always wanted one," Lucy said, her voice breaking. "I'm going to be the best big sister you could ever have." She slumped onto Nana's lap with Sara.

Nana was talking softly as she cleared Sara's tear-dampened hair away from her face. "I'll come to see you regularly, and when you have vacation from school, you'll come back to the farm, yes you will, Sara." Putting her hands on Sara's shoulders and sitting her up straight, she continued, "There are just so many more children here in Silver Spring for you to play with. You would get lonely if you stayed at the farm." Slowly Sara turned around to look at all of us. She let Lucy lift her from Nana's lap onto hers and cuddle her.

"We're going to have so much fun, Sara. I'll get all my dolls out for you to play with, and the dollhouse. It was Mom's and Auntie Netts's dollhouse, you know. I think you're going to like it here, sister of mine."

David got up and asked if anyone was interested in making ice cream sundaes. "I'll help," Sara yelled, scrambling down off Lucy's lap and running into the kitchen after David.

When I put her to bed later, I stayed with her as she fell asleep, singing the same lullaby I'd sung the other two:

> Sail baby sail
> Far across the sea
> Only don't forget to come
> Back again to me.

> Baby's fishing for a dream
> Fishing near and far
> Her line a silver moonbeam is
> Her bait a silver star

The next morning, Sara appeared at our bedside before six.

"Morning, Sara. How's our girl this morning?" I asked, putting my arms out to help her onto the bed with us.

"What are we having for breakfast this morning, Mom?" she said, snuggling next to me.

I nudged David under the covers. *Mom! I'd already made it into her lexicon as Mom.*

We engaged a family therapist to help shepherd us through this transition. Cherry advised each of us weekly on how to relate to the vast changes Sara's arrival had brought about in the family. She worked with Sara to uncover the impact of what she'd been through and to teach her the skills she'd need to handle each issue as it came along.

For me, Sara's arrival seemed to be a healing—and certainly a new direction. I loved being with her. When I held her close to me, I could feel our bodies offering each other a warmth and trust we both needed in our lives just then. On weekends we took naps with our bodies glued together. At the pool where I swam each morning, we spent hours playing in the water, Sara hanging onto me tightly. The third crease the palmist had seen on my hand turned out to be a beautiful, intelligent, intensely curious little girl.

Sara found my box collection fascinating. More than once I'd come upon her in my room, a chair pulled up to the dresser, arranging and re-arranging the boxes, opening them and trying on the jewelry inside. One day our dog Hazel greeted me at the door wearing one of my mother's clip-on earrings.

Another day I pulled into the driveway after work to find nearly a quarter of the big front lawn under a make-shift tent, sticks holding up sheets that had been tied together. While my instructions to the babysitter were to encourage Sara's "amazing creativity," emptying out the linen closet of every single sheet and towel was perhaps a little too creative. I patiently spoke with the sitter about the need to undertake "reasonable" projects.

Not long after the tent came a cooking phase. I returned from work to find Sara standing on the bench, leaning over the huge stainless pot I used for canning. Inside was a "magic potion," and she was adding one new ingredient after another. I very evenly asked if she was working from a recipe.

"My mom said the best things came when you made them up," she said. "This has dirt, corn meal, marigolds, salt and pepper, and some red food coloring." The counter was covered with globs of potion. Sara's school clothes had splotches of red food coloring all over them.

"I think you have to remember to wear an apron next time. And let's remember not to taste this potion. That dirt might make you sick."

Discovering the back porch completely covered in an aluminum foil installation later the same week nearly tipped me back into my old ways.

"Sara," I said, taking a deep breath, "whatever inspired you to carpet the back porch with foil? I don't think we'll be able to use any of this foil again, and it's really pretty expensive, you know."

"I don't like it when you scream at me," she said, blotches breaking out on her adorable face and tears welling in her eyes.

"I wasn't screaming, Sara," I said calmly. "I was just a little unhappy." I really wasn't screaming, and I was proud of myself for it. But Sara apparently could tell when I *wanted* to scream.

That night we sat down on the bench together in the kitchen and brainstormed the first "Sara's Anti-bored List." We used shelf paper so it could be as long as it needed to be. Sara chose the color of marker we used, and we both came up with ideas:

1. Make jello.
2. Paint a picture on the easel.
3. Weed the garden.
4. Sweep the kitchen floor.
5. Work the cross-stitch for Nana's present.

As the list unfolded, Sara decorated each entry with pictures. She wanted to add doing the laundry, but I reminded her that was Dad's job that he liked to do Saturday mornings. When we were done, there were more than thirty suggestions for staving off boredom. We posted it on the cellar door, for easy reference should the urge to decorate the porch floor or similar projects come over her again.

When the ideas on the Anti-bored List no longer appealed to her, Sara came up with new ones. The summer she was seven, we discovered she had a flair for enterprise.

One day at the height of the garden season, I arrived home and was astonished to discover not one single flower blooming in the garden.

"Sara, did you pick lots of flowers this afternoon?" I inquired in as nonchalant a voice as I could muster. "This morning it looked like everything was blooming, and this afternoon it looks kinda empty."

"Four whole bouquets! And I sold all of them. Isn't that great?" she said.

"*Sold* them! To whom?" I was astonished.

"To Helen Ann, the Browns, the Wolcotts, Charlie . . . They thought they were beautiful," she said with pride.

The following week we got a call from our neighbors, the Browns. "Is there any chance my shoes could be ready for an important meeting tomorrow morning?" Fred asked.

"Your shoes? I'm not sure I can help you, Fred."

"Well, Sara came around yesterday afternoon with her wagon collecting our shoes. Said she'd launched a shoe shine business and wondered if we had any shoes that needed to be polished. We gave her all we had," he said enthusiastically.

"Wow," I said, taking a deep breath. "I guess I didn't know about this particular scheme. Let me check and get back to you, Fred. And thanks for your support."

"Sara," I called upstairs. "Sara, come tell me about the shoe shine business. Fred Brown needs his tomorrow. Are they ready?" I asked, trying to sound unruffled by this initiative.

"There're so many shoes out there, I don't know which ones are Fred's, that's the problem," she said, leaning over the banister, her thick brown hair hanging in her face.

"Can you show me where the shop is?" I asked, lifting my voice to indicate happy interest.

Sara descended the steps and led me outside to the garage, where a heap of maybe twenty-two pairs of shoes lay scattered helter-skelter in the center of the cement floor. David's very elementary shoe-shine kit lay off to one side.

"A lot of people wanted their shoes shined," she said. "Isn't this exciting? I'm going to get lots of money like you and Dad do at work."

"Well, yes, I guess it is exciting, but you don't really *need* to earn money, Sara. We have plenty of money for what we need. But, listen, don't you think it would be good if you knew whose shoes were whose and which ones had to be done when? I didn't know you'd switched from flowers to shoes."

"We didn't really have enough flowers, so I decided on the shoe shine. Dad showed me how."

"Dad showed you how to shine shoes?" I asked in as even a voice as I could, trying not to laugh, which is what I really wanted to do.

"Yup. And I've already gotten some pay. She went to an orange crate in the back of the garage and fished out the "money box." It had come directly from my dresser, and ironically, it was the Mexican tin box her own mother had sent me for Christmas years before.

Sara's first Christmas at our house, Lucy put herself in charge of orienting her to the traditions we observe, beginning with the arrival of the Advent calendars on December First, with a chocolate behind the window for each day. "Remember, Sara, only one chocolate a day," Lucy counseled her.

Two days later, Lucy met me at the door when I arrived home with the news that Sara had been really "bad." "What did she do?" I asked, concerned.

"She ate every last chocolate in her Advent calendar. Can you believe it?" she asked in a most disgusted tone.

"Lucy, let it go. It's not that important. Tell you what, why don't you take her Christmas shopping? You two can ride the little bus, shop around some and be home in time for a late dinner."

"Super idea, Mom."

Sara's first Christmas became *Sara's* Christmas. Every Christmas since, it's been recounted, especially by her siblings. It seemed that packages came for her from everyone who'd ever met her or heard about her. The usual stack of presents under our two-story tree grew taller than ever. Christmas morning, Sara, Lucy, Nana and I all descended to the living room in our matching red Lanz nighties.

"They're all for Sara," Lucy said a little petulantly.

"Lucy, it's not her fault."

"Sara, you're going to make it into *Ripley's Believe It or Not,*" Marsh said.

"Lucy, you can help me unwrap," Sara said. We all smiled at her thoughtfulness.

When the unwrapping was nearly done, Sara got up from where she was sitting and ran upstairs. "What's the matter?" I called.

"Nothing. I just forgot something. I mean, Santa forgot something," she called down.

Holding up her nightie with one hand, she barreled down the stairs holding a small, wrapped gift aloft. "Here, Mom."

She climbed into my lap. "It's just what you needed," she said. I opened it slowly. A little round Chinese silk box. The bottom was black silk, the top bright red with golden flowers embroidered into the fabric.

"It's for the top of your dresser, Mom. For your pearls!"

"Sara, it's the most beautiful box I've ever gotten. Thank you so much," I said, giving her a big hug and kiss. Two days earlier, I'd come home to find her wearing those very pearls—and I hadn't even been tempted to scream.

❧

When Sara was thirteen, our lives once again changed dramatically. I was appointed Peace Corps Country Director in Belize, charged with supporting the work of 100 American volunteers. Lucy was at the University of Chicago, Marshall was planting trees, and Sara found herself alone with us in a foreign country. Our enthusiasm for the challenge of living overseas was matched only by her lack of enthusiasm at that point for nearly everything we said or did. We'd been warned that Sara's teen years could be particularly challenging, given the emotional trauma she'd suffered. I worried that dragging her off to completely new surroundings and a new culture would only add to that potential.

Sara enrolled at St. Catherine Academy, run by the Sisters of Mercy, in Belize City next door to my office. Wearing a uniform, making friends, and avoiding getting demerits were all challenging. But she got high grades on her first report card, which we figured was an encouraging sign. And we tried to help with the friends.

"Sara, guess what? The Ambassador and his family are coming over tonight. His son is exactly your age and very cute."

"Mom, I'm not interested in meeting the Ambassador's son."

"C'mon, Sara. Maybe you two can talk about how much you hate your parents for bringing you here," I suggested. "You both definitely have that in common."

While the parents chatted animatedly, Sara sat on one side of the room, the Ambassador's son on the other side. Both remained silent throughout the evening. So much for that strategy.

Then I heard about Rosita Arvigo's garden in a town not far from us. Maybe this would help bring Sara out of her funk. An American naturopath transplanted to Belize, Rosita was trained by her ancient Mayan neighbor to take over his healing practice. She had a huge garden of herbs she used in tinctures and tonics, an active healing practice, and she was ready for some help.

"Sara could come out here this summer, live with us and work in the garden," she suggested.

"Rosita, this is a wonderful idea. Sara's an incredibly hard worker, and maybe you can give her a tincture that will lift her spirits."

Sara seemed surprisingly enthusiastic about going to work with Rosita. She'd always loved to garden.

"That's great, Mom. But I don't know what all those plants are," she said.

"Don't worry. Rosita will teach you. Maybe she'll even treat you for the Belize Blues."

"Mom. That's not funny."

When we picked Sara up at the end of the summer, we found a new young woman. She was brighter, happier and full of enthusiasm for all she'd learned. In the meantime David and I had discussed the fact that she wasn't getting enough of the academic subjects she'd need to apply to college in the US. How would she feel about applying to boarding schools back in the States, we asked. Peace Corps would pay her tuition, and she might be happier there than at St. Catherine's. Sara jumped at the chance. Reluctantly we saw her off to her choice, George School, just outside Philadelphia.

With high grades at graduation, high SAT scores and success in the International Baccalaureate program, Sara's prospects for college were good. She was an artist whose wood-working skills were the envy of people twice her age. She was an accomplished athlete. Despite all these assets, I was still concerned about the application process. I brought it up with her on the phone.

"How are your college application essays going, Sara?"

"Don't worry, Mom. I'll get them done," she said confidently.

"But, Sara . . . . they count for a lot. Don't you think it would be good to brainstorm some ideas?"

"I'll send you a copy when I'm finished," she responded.

I continued to worry. *Was it a mistake to drag her down to Belize at such a critical age? Maybe sending her off to boarding school had been hard on her.*

The following week an envelope arrived. No note from Sara, just two essays and the instructions from the Common Application: The first essay was to be on a formative experience. *What had she written about?* I sunk into the sofa to read.

"Moving to Belize changed my life dramatically," was the opening line. *Uh-oh. This could be bad news.* "Suddenly I had to find my own way in a new culture and see myself reflected in others' eyes . . . I didn't know the language . . . I didn't have any friends . . .

"It also marked the beginning of my career as an organic gardener . . . I had the privilege of being an intern for a Mayan healer who taught me how to recognize, grow and harvest important plants . . . Teaching others the importance of gardening will always be part of my life . . . "

Tears rolled down my cheeks. I phoned David to read the essay to him. Sara would be okay. I had been okay. What we'd done raising her was good. Her mother Susan might even be proud of me. How I wish she could know that her daughter, with a degree in environmental sciences and a masters in sustainability, now teaches residents of Lehigh County, Pennsylvania, how to be farmers.

The palmist was right—I did take on big jobs, in this case my promise to myself that I would be a patient mother to Sara and offer her the opportunities she needed to become herself. My third child had proven to be not only Susan's last gift to our family but also a gift to me of myself.

CHAPTER ELEVEN

Irreplaceable

Our big brown riding bear lay on top of the heap. All oily and muddy. When David heaved him onto the pile awaiting the front-end loader, I completely lost it. One Christmas Eve when we were visiting, my father had arrived home proudly carrying that huge stuffed bear with red wheels. Driving by FAO Schwarz in Ardmore on his way out from the city, he'd seen it in the window. As a child Daddy had received one for Christmas himself from the very same store, and so he'd bought a replica for his youngest grandson. And now, there was Bear, soggy, slimy, his fur completely matted, atop the pile of floor boards David had torn up. We were on the fifth day of clean-up after 1972's Tropical Storm Agnes. It had hit our city hard. I was running on empty, and this reminder of Daddy, also lost to us, was putting me over the top.

We'd been living in Harrisburg, Pennsylvania, for scarcely three months. Although the forecast had predicted a hundred-year flood, no one we talked to had ever heard of the river coming up as far as our house. We thought riding out the rainstorm would be like getting through a winter blizzard—something we'd done plenty of times. It had always meant cozy gatherings with friends and family. So the night the flood was due to arrive—somewhere else we were sure—we invited friends over. We'd eat, we'd play bridge, we'd drink. It never occurred to me that the rising waters would have anything to do with us.

We loved our new neighborhood and our first "owned" home. Steve and Geri in the other half of our duplex had become family in short order. They had a daughter, Alisa, who fit neatly between Marsh and Lucy. And Mrs. Fisher on the other side of our house had adopted Lucy as her own.

"Will you be hiring a helicopter to clean your front window?" Mrs. Fisher had asked the first time we met. Our house had a leaded glass window spanning two of its three stories.

"Maybe," I'd laughed, introducing myself and Lucy, who at two-and-a-half seemed nearly as tall as our tiny neighbor. A bit stooped and very white-haired, Mrs. Fisher walked with a distinct limp. Ignoring my suggestion that she shake our neighbor's hand, Lucy toddled over and gave her leg a hug. Clearly delighted, Mrs. Fisher put an affectionate hand around Lucy's head.

I was unprepared for what came next. I reached out to shake Mrs. Fisher's hand and cupped it warmly in both of mine. There on the inside of her forearm, amidst a network of veins, was a tattooed number. A *tattooed number.* For a split second, my blue eyes met her dark eyes. Mrs. Fisher must be a Holocaust survivor. My mind flashed back to photos I'd seen in *Life* magazine as a child and the horror I felt as I read the stories over and over again. Here was someone right next door who'd lived through that. She must have lost everything, maybe *everyone.* I searched her eyes to see if any of that sorrow was obvious there. She looked away.

"Mrs. Fisher, I think you have a good idea for cleaning this window," I'd said, breaking the silence. "We'll remember the helicopter when we get to that part of working on the house."

Lucy and I had watched her as she turned to limp home.

Lucy was the early riser at our house, which meant we rarely needed an alarm clock. Starting almost exactly at six everyday, we'd hear her reading aloud—from memory. Some mornings she'd be totally engaged with her dolls, "reading" to them or telling them stories about Marshall or other events in her life. The morning after we met Mrs. Fisher, we woke up to silence.

Where was Lucy? Not in her room. Maybe downstairs watching television or getting herself some Cheerios? No sign of her. I started to panic. As I came back through the living room, running to alert David, I noticed the front door ajar. Stepping outside, I was met with the vision of Mrs. Fisher and Lucy coming across the yard hand in hand, Lucy in her nightgown, Mrs. Fisher in her bathrobe.

"I heard a knocking at the door and here came my little princess," Mrs. Fisher's voice swelled with delight. "She was so chilly, I just put her in bed with me."

For three days before our blizzard party, we'd been hearing news on the radio about the possibility of a hundred-year flood. The rain was relentless. The ground was sodden. Sidewalks were slippery. The last days of the school year had been cancelled. Most businesses were closed, and I'd made plans to stay home from work. But early on the morning of the fourth rainy day in a row, my boss called to say he needed me to help publicize which schools the Red Cross would be opening as evacuation centers.

Hoping to lure our secretary into work with the promise of chocolate, I set about making a quick batch of brownies. More than a few of them remained at home with the kids and our neighbor Geri, who'd volunteered to babysit. Braving the downpour, David and I and made our way downtown. Even though the wipers were going at top speed, we could barely see. I dropped him at the Capitol, where he worked as a reporter for the Pittsburgh *Post-Gazette,* and headed for the basement parking lot of my office building. Water had blown in, and the concrete floor looked icy. As I got out of the car, cradling the plate of brownies, my pocketbook and my notebook, my foot slipped and I went into a slide. My left ankle twisted under me as I fell, and shards of the broken brownie plate cut my hand open as I tried to catch myself. Blood and brownies were everywhere. Not another soul was around to hear me scream—not in pain but in frustration, fear and absolute fury

I crawled into the elevator, dragging my already swelling ankle. On my knees I reached for the telephone, proud of myself for remembering there would be one there.

"David, come quick. I've had a fall, and I think we probably should go to the hospital. I'm really sorry. It's my ankle, and I'm bleeding."

"Deedie, where are you?"

"I'm in the elevator," I said, beginning to cry. "In the garage. This is so dumb. Why, why am I always getting myself into pickles like this?" David had already hung up and was on his way.

Seeing firsthand how a hospital begins to prepare for a natural disaster would have been more fascinating had I not been one of its first victims. I was relieved to know my ankle wasn't broken, but then a surgeon arrived to work on my thumb, which was badly cut.

He turned on the tap to wash his hands. Nothing came out. "They said this could happen if our supply system got overwhelmed," he announced. That the city was in a bona fide emergency was beginning to sink in. I was dismayed that I was having my own personal version of it rather than being part of the response team.

News reports on the television continued to predict that this night would signal the beginning of the biggest flood since 1936, maybe before. Rain and more rain was forecast. Lying on the sofa in front of the big window with my leg propped up and my left hand pointing skyward, I watched the rain coming down so hard I could hear it hitting the sodden ground outside. We might not need that helicopter for window cleaning after all.

Mrs. Fisher came over, a tiny heap under her big blue umbrella with purple irises on it. "I'm coming to say good-bye before I leave for high ground," she declared breathlessly as she stepped inside. "What in heaven's name have you done to yourself?" she asked when she caught sight of me. "How will you take care of these children in the middle of a flood?"

"Oh, I just had a little accident. Stupid, I know. We don't think we're going to get the water. Where did you hear we were?" I asked.

"Oh it's what everyone's talking about. I'm quite surprised you don't know," she said.

"I guess they'll tell us if we have to leave, but it doesn't seem like it," I replied, confident for some unknown reason.

"Well, good-bye. You take care of yourself." Mrs. Fisher gave Lucy a big hug and kiss and left. I watched her carefully avoid walking on the swampy grass.

Despite the dire warnings, David continued with his party preparations. The makings for gin and tonics. Extra leaves in Granny's table for the bridge game. Geri was cooking a Brunswick stew to bring over. The rain continued coming down so hard that when the kids ran the ten feet between the back doors of our duplex, they had to wear their raincoats.

It was around eight o'clock, the children had just gone to bed, and we were starting to deal the cards for bridge when we heard a banging at the front door. David opened it to find a fireman, encased in yellow rubber from top to bottom. In the distance, sirens were blaring.

"Okay, folks. You're being evacuated. We need you to get out as soon as you can. The river's coming up fast, and we expect this whole neighborhood to be under water this time tomorrow. We don't have much time. Let's get you moving."

"But, sir, can't we just stay?" I said, hopping toward the door. "We just got our kids to bed. We have dogs. And we have a second floor. Are you *sure* we're in danger?"

"What I'm sure of, m'am, is you have to leave. We've opened several of the schools here in your neighborhood for you to go to. (*As if I didn't know!*) You need to begin leaving now, while you can," he said politely.

Steve and Geri rushed out the back door to get what they could from their house. David woke the children. I called some friends to say we were coming. There would be six of us—and no dogs. They would stay upstairs, and we'd get them the next day.

By the time we closed the front door, we could hear an ominous gurgling in all the drains. We had no idea they would soon be the pipeline through which the Susquehanna River would flow, into the very first house we'd ever owned. David opened the basement door to find that water already covered the second step. How could all this have happened so quickly?

Sopping wet, David and I squeezed into our aging Volvo alongside two sleepy children, their pillows and our guests. Steve, Geri and Alisa preceded us in their own vehicle to their friends' house. The honking blast from the radio's emergency warning system filled the car the minute the engine turned over. This was not a test. The Mayor's nasal voice broke in: "I've ordered a full evacuation of the Uptown area. The river is rising swiftly, and all citizens must move out of their houses immediately. Front Street. Second Street. Green Street . . . . ," he went on naming our whole neighborhood.

The new word in our vocabulary became "crest." Now that it was clear the river was rising at unprecedented speed, the big question was, "When would it crest?" We turned on our hosts' television at the beginning of each hour to hear the latest. Forecast after forecast predicted a long wait. After two nights and no crest in sight, we said goodbye to our friends and left for my brother Bill's house in suburban Philadelphia, where a family gathering was underway. There was no telling how long we would have to camp out.

While the rain was no longer coming down in sheets, it was still coming down. We arrived at Bill's house wearing the same clothes we'd left our own house in three days earlier. I was on crutches, wearing one shoe, a soiled sock stretched over my injured ankle.

We were stopped in the foyer by the "welcoming committee"—my mother, Bill, Bill's wife Walton, *her* mother and my sister Nettie, all of whom began pummeling us with questions. What had we done with all the family treasures? Had we brought the silver with us? Did we move the china upstairs? What about the rugs? Did we put the paintings and the punch bowl in safe places? The furniture—where had we moved it? Where was Granny's dining room table? Where are your clothes, your suitcases? Lucy, dear, your dress is *filthy*. Here, let me take it off right now. Donnan, where *is* your other shoe?

I don't remember if there were any hugs.

I took a deep breath. Lucy handed me her dress, and she and Marsh went off to play with their cousins. I took another deep breath. I looked around at all of them. They weren't looking at me. They were talking among themselves, reminding each other of items at our flooded house they'd forgotten to ask about. I held onto David, then leaned against the wall to get my balance, taking another deep breath. Completely unannounced, the words came coursing through my body and onto my tongue—so quickly I didn't have time to edit them.

"Here's the answer to all those questions you have. I thought *we* were more important than all those things. I'll give all those *things* back if that's what you want. As to what happens to the house, who knows? Maybe we'll have a house, maybe we won't. We didn't know we were going to be evacuated. We got out of there with the children's pillows and that's all. David and Steve went back the next day in a boat to get the dogs off the second-floor balconies." I was shaking now and Bill was holding up his hand as if he were on the safety patrol.

My mother was muttering, "Honestly, Donnan, really. No need for Sarah Bernhardt here."

But I was undaunted. "Did anyone ask me how my leg and hand are? 'No,' is the answer to that. It may seem stupid to you but I was actually hurt trying to get to work. But you all seem to be much more interested in punch bowls and paintings. That's the message I'm getting. That's the message I've always gotten."

Walton said, "Maybe you ought to sit down, Donnan. I bet you'd be more comfortable." It was getting more and more awkward to have all of us crowded into the entryway. I was no longer shaking though. I was beginning to feel a whole new world open up to me. I shifted my crutches to the same side.

"Can you all hear me? Listen to this. If anyone asks us one more question about one more thing, we will leave, depart, and never return. We have many, many good friends. They care about what happens to us. Hear me when I say I don't give a tinker's damn about our things. Especially now. Am I happy to be their steward? Yes. But they definitely play second fiddle to people in our life."

I was done. My face was flushed, and all I wanted to do was smile. Smile at having gotten something articulated that I clearly had been feeling for a while. How else could I have come up with such a sermon on the spot? Was this the family version of speaking in tongues?

Bill patted my arm and turned to go into the living room. My mother broke the silence. "I'm ready for a good stiff drink," she said, following Bill.

I was thirty-one years old, and it felt like I had come of age, at a time and moment no one could have predicted, especially not me. Every now and then during the rest of our stay at Bill and Walton's, I'd come upon someone having a whispered conversation about what might happen to all the submerged heirlooms. But no one said another word to us again about *things.*

Two days later, David and I drove back to Harrisburg. About three inches of slime and mud covered the streets and sidewalks. When we got to the front door, we couldn't get it open. Swollen to nearly twice its thickness with river water, it only yielded when David heaved his whole body against it.

Inside the house was just as muddy as outside. The watermarks on the walls and windows were at about four and a half feet. Our heating oil tank had overturned downstairs, and the smell of oil was everywhere. The furniture was mostly where it belonged, having been picked up as the water came up and laid down gently as it drained out. But the coffee table where I'd left my gin and tonic had floated the length of the living room, coming to rest at the fireplace, the glass exactly where I left it. The kitchen was covered with a light brown layer of something awful I feared, until I realized it was the twenty-five-pound bag of dog food, unleashed. The cookbooks and recipe box had floated off the shelf, forming a layer of their own. A small fish lay dead near the back door.

"Whew. I never understood before what flood victims go through," I said to no one. David had wandered off to the basement. I thought back to my only other flood experience, at twelve years old with my father, when he'd accused me of not being sympathetic enough. *I wasn't.*

"Look at this. The 'fridge has been up-ended, but not the washer and dryer," David called up. I stood at the top of the steps, looking down at the children's toys encased in mud. The bear on wheels lay on his side, his brown fur matted and slimy. I didn't have the heart to mention our sodden wedding album to David.

The water had only gone up several of the stairs to the second floor, so up there everything looked normal. Our bedroom was exactly as we'd left it, except for the balcony door they'd forced open when they came to get Leonard Cohen, our dog. I looked at the collection of boxes on my dresser and wondered how I would have felt if they'd been swept away. I thought about each one and the people who'd given them. Boxes or no boxes, those people would remain alive and well inside my head and heart. I'd learned from my own speech in Bill's foyer that *things*, important as they are, could all be let go.

While our nights were spent upstairs, our daytime headquarters were in the front yard for the next two months or so. Each day's pile of broken furniture and detritus awaited the city's dump trucks. Up and down the street, the scene was the same. Houses and yards were hosed down nearly every day for a week.

Our neighborhood became our family. We shared meals. We shared tasks. We shared volunteers—and tears, which tended to make appearances when you least expected them. Volunteers came from all over the country. The Mennonite Disaster Service Corps sent people our way, fresh from another flood in Rapid City, South Dakota, carrying their own mops, buckets, rubber gloves and Clorox. The Red Cross brought sandwiches every day, gave us enough cash to buy cleaning materials, and a list of what to buy. The Small Business Administration set up offices and offered help with our mortgages and low-interest recovery loans. Friends from other cities called to say they'd be coming over the weekend to pitch in.

One day I looked up to see a well-dressed older man coming toward our house. David was right behind him. Who was it?

"You must be Deedie. I'm Bill Block." I shook his hand, and the next thing I knew he was giving me a hug. Bill Block! He was the owner of the *Post-Gazette*. David's big boss. He'd actually flown in from Pittsburgh just to see how we were doing.

"David's firsthand stories about being a flood victim have been sensational," he said, "But I had to see for myself."

We gave him a tour of the house. We introduced him to the neighbors. We told him our plans for reconstruction, once everything had dried out.

"We didn't really know how we could help, but I figured you could use this," he said, putting a big wad of money in my hand. "I heard the banks were under water too."

This was my first experience with absolute untrammeled generosity, and with hundred dollar bills. I couldn't help thinking back to my own family's reaction to our situation and how different it was.

Mrs. Fisher had joined the group of people gathered to meet Mr. Block.

"Where's my little girl?" she wanted to know.

"We left her in Philadelphia with our family," I told her.

"Did you lose a lot too, Mrs. Fisher?" Mr. Block asked her.

"Oh I didn't lose anything I can't replace," she said. "My living room suite, my bedroom suite, the kitchen, everything . . . ." she recited the lost inventory of her one-story house. "I was hoping their little girl Lucy and I could have a tea party out here under the dogwood tree this afternoon."

Mrs. Fisher was right. Every*thing* in the house was replaceable. And no matter what we had lost, memories of tea parties with a little blonde girl and of a father who brought a Christmas riding bear to his grandson would never float away.

CHAPTER TWELVE

Meritorious Increase

"Miss Deedie. The *Ambassador's* on his way up to your office." The receptionist's voice sounded urgent, nervous.

I was in Belize City, on the third floor of the seaside colonial mansion that housed Peace Corps/Belize. It was the usual sweltering day in the tropics.

"What did he say?" I asked, trying not to sound too concerned.

"All he said was 'Hello, I'm going to see Mrs. Runkel.' I couldn't stop him, really I couldn't."

"Not to worry," I reassured her.

Before the Ambassador had finished climbing the three flights to my floor, news of his on-site visit had coursed through the building. My phone rang again. It was George.

"Are you sure everything's okay, Deedie?"

"We'll just wait to see what he has to say," I said in a hushed tone. "I'm sure it's about my not signing that mammoth document they brought over last week, the one justifying hardship pay for all the Americans."

"Good luck," George said.

As we hung up, the Ambassador appeared at my door. I got up to welcome him. He'd arrived in Belize about the same time I did, a few months before, and he'd made a point of telling me how noble the Peace Corps' work was and that he had every intention of respecting the arm's-length relationship between it and the U.S. State Department. As I soon noticed, there was more than an arm's-length difference in how the two agencies operated. In my mind the Hardship Pay Justification was a perfect example. It set out all the reasons why Americans who work in Belize should get a twenty-five percent differential added to their pay because of all they had to endure living in a developing country.

"Deedie! Madam Director," the Ambassador greeted me, pausing to catch his breath. "Too bad you don't have an elevator here. But wow, what a view."

"Isn't it great? I get to watch all the action on the sea, the children in the play yard at St. Catherine's and the USAID parking lot. Not bad," I said.

He was actually carrying the Hardship Pay Justification document, approximately four inches thick. No wonder he was out of breath. When it had first been presented for my signature as the head of an American government agency, I'd declined, saying it was irrelevant since Peace Corps personnel didn't get the differential. Besides, I didn't think working in Belize was a hardship. Between my first refusal and this moment, I'd been lobbied by the Ambassador's deputy and by the USAID director to 'just go ahead and sign."

But as I leafed through the pages of the document, I'd become even more resistant. It catalogued the perceived hardships: No cultural activities in Belize. It was very hot and one could get malaria, Dengue Fever or be bitten by poisonous snakes. The water wasn't potable. There were open sewers. Healthcare wasn't reliable. Neither was electricity. I felt embarrassed that

Belizeans would even know we had these negative thoughts, let alone that the American Embassy had been involved in preparing such a treatise.

"This isn't a battle worth fighting," the Ambassador's deputy had said.

"No battle coming from me," I said. "It just isn't relevant to Peace Corps. All of those conditions are exactly why we're here. Right?"

"Maybe you. Not me," he'd replied.

The Ambassador pulled a chair up to my desk, plunking the document down there. Of course, he thought I'd be sitting behind my desk. Instead, I pulled a chair up next to him. Ordinarily, I would have found such a visit intimidating. That day, I felt confident and clear.

"So, Mr. Ambassador, I gather that my not signing this document has ruffled some feathers," I ventured.

"Well, the head of every American agency is *required* to sign it. That's why I brought it with me today. I know you're new to foreign service, but this is how it works. You see that slot there, it says *Peace Corps Director*. That's you. I don't want to be a bully about this, but I did promise you I'd show you the ropes when necessary after you admitted you were a rookie at our first meeting," he said, smiling and winking at me.

"Well, I do see that the Peace Corps is listed there, Mr. Ambassador. But as you know, we do not benefit in any way from the Hardship Pay Differential, so I see no reason why I should have to sign it. I'd be very surprised if my not signing it affected anyone else getting that 25 percent." I wanted to spew forth about how outrageous I found it that the taxpayers were going to have to pay all that money to staff for living in a country where annually 250,000 Americans spent their vacations.

"Deedie, let me give you a good piece of advice. This is not an issue worth taking a stand on. Why don't you just sign your name and we'll be able to move forward? You don't want to do anything to jeopardize your career, I'm sure," he said, leaning over for emphasis.

"You know, Mr. Ambassador, I have no worries whatsoever about how this may affect my career. I know I was sent down here to a troubled post because I'm considered an effective, principled manager. Right now I have 100 Americans here as volunteers and more than a few messes left over from the last director to clean up. I've got a plan in place and a staff to help me. I feel quite certain that when it comes time to evaluate my performance, whether or not I have signed this justification is not going to figure into the equation." I could feel color rising in my cheeks and nerve-induced perspiration flowing under my arms, but I couldn't help being impressed with how confident I sounded.

He patted my knee as he got up. "Unfortunately for you, Deedie, this is probably not the last you're going to hear about this issue, whether you want to or not," he said, shaking hands.

"I'm sure there'll be lots of things on which we'll see eye to eye further down the road," I said. "Thanks for coming down the lane to see me."

"You need to get yourself some air conditioning," he said, taking his handkerchief out of his pocket and wiping his brow.

"Are you kidding? With the sea breeze flowing in here all day, I wouldn't think of it. I hope that's not an order," I said, giving him a little wink and a giggle.

The Ambassador had been the least of my worries when I arrived as Country Director of Peace Corps/Belize. I couldn't imagine what the Belizean staff were expecting from a new director. The past four hadn't lasted long, and the one just before me had attracted the attention of the Inspector General of Peace Corps. My assignment was what some in Washington called a "rescue" mission. It was hard enough to be a Peace Corps director, but following a few bad acts made it all the more daunting.

It had been arranged for me to be met on my arrival at the airport by a local associate director, Dorothy, who'd been with Peace Corps/Belize since it started nearly thirty years earlier. Emerging from Customs with my huge over-stuffed Land's End red duffel hanging from my shoulder, I was struggling to maintain balance and control of everything I was carrying. Someone called my name.

"Mrs. Runkel. Here I am. Deedie! Is that you?"

Dorothy came to my side, holding out a hand. I clumsily stretched out my left hand since it was the only one free.

Her wispy grey hair was contained by bastions of silver bobby pins that marched down the back of her head to the nape of her neck. Her dress was loose and formless, her face without make-up. At nearly sixty, she was considered an elder in this society where a shorter average lifespan meant that people tended to retire in their fifties. Her skin was light enough to pass for white, but in Belize I knew she would be known as a Creole—a designation reserved for those whose forebears were an acknowledged amalgam that might include British emigrants, pirates, English loggers, shipwrecked African slaves or some combination of all of them.

Dorothy drove me to the "Director's House," a two-story pink concrete affair a block from the sea, the run-down, unpainted wall around it lined with royal palms and bright red canna lilies. I'd been in Peace Corps Directors' houses in a half-dozen countries, and this one looked a little shabby in comparison. Never mind, I would make it grand. Dorothy gave me her phone number and said to call her if I needed anything.

The first thing I did was to rip off my beastly hot panty hose. Sliding into shorts, I surveyed the house, looking for the best spot for each thing I'd carefully calculated I'd need for this first month by myself. Summer clothes in November. All cotton to keep me cooler. The essential coffee bean grinder and pot. Two bathing suits. (My daily early-morning swims could be outside here.) Towels. Sun screen. Boots for hiking out to see volunteers living in the remote bush. I deposited in the 'fridge the two massive turkeys I'd brought for the Thanksgiving dinner the Director traditionally puts on for volunteers.

My brief encounter with Dorothy had seemed cordial and given me confidence that I would be accepted on my first foreign assignment. I was excited to finally be on the frontlines of Peace Corps after five years of working at headquarters. That put a flush on my face, a combination of relief and growing excitement for the adventure. I felt like everything I'd ever done had led up to this moment.

Belize had a reputation for having too many volunteers doing too little. I'd been sent to do something about that. There were five associate directors, each supervising the program in a specific section of the country and overseeing about twenty volunteers. Peace Corps headquarters had declared that every volunteer must have a real job, and each agency or school involved must be a strong, participating partner in its local program. So before arriving, I'd told the associate directors I wanted to visit each section of the country and every volunteer during my first month.

To my delight, detailed plans and dates for trips were on my desk my very first day—from four of the five associate directors. Where were Dorothy's plans? My first call on the inter-office phone was to Extension 19.

"Dorothy! It's Deedie. Thanks so much for helping me get settled yesterday. It's great to feel so welcomed. Now, tell me when are we going to go see some of your volunteers?"

"We're going tomorrow, Mrs. Runkel. We'll be leaving at 8:30 from your house. I'll pick you up. Will that be okay with you?"

"Oh, yes. Yes. That's just great. I just didn't know for sure. I have everyone else's travel plans and hadn't seen yours."

"I'll tell you in person everything you need to know," she said. "Not to worry. No problem, I'm sure."

"What shall I wear, Dorothy? Where exactly are we going?"

"I think we'll go on out to Double Head Cabbage and Lucky Strike. Those are two good villages for you to see. We have a volunteer in one of them, and a REAP school in the other where the volunteer sometimes works. We'll go there, no problem," she said. It sounded to me strangely like the more she talked, the more certain of her plans she became. "You can just wear your office clothes. That's what I'll be wearing." Even the most naïve new director could tell that were it not for my call, Dorothy's plan might not have been hatched.

The next day as we rumbled along the corduroy road to Double Head Cabbage, Dorothy gave me the promised briefing of everything I needed to know about our upcoming visit to a school there. I shouldn't be put off by the fact, she told me, that the principal was pretty headstrong and actually didn't like Peace Corps very much. The volunteer we were headed out to see wasn't always at her post; she was supposed to be an agricultural volunteer, but the principal thought he'd like to have her teach reading instead. The local education officer in the District was often drunk, she went on, so it was best to meet with him before lunch, which we might not make. And the other volunteer was with the Youth Enhancement Program, which was just another one of those programs like so many we'd tried in the past. *Did she sound cynical?* I began to wonder just whose side she was on.

"Wow, Dorothy. It must be pretty discouraging some days, with all these challenges you have," I said.

"Oh no, Miss Deedie. That's just the way Peace Corps is. You'll find out. Here we are in Double Head Cabbage."

Mr. Fanning, the principal who wasn't a fan of the Peace Corps, appeared to be leaving. Dorothy went over to his shiny red Honda scooter and talked with him a minute or two. At length, they came over to where I stood near the car.

"How do you do, Mr. Fanning. I'm Deedie Runkel. How nice of you to let us visit your school."

"Mrs. Runkel is the new Peace Corps Director, as I was telling you, Mr. Fanning," Dorothy said. "We're just checking in so she can see where the volunteers work.

"I understand you have the REAP program here," I said, "the *Rural Education Agricultural Program?*" I was speaking fast, as it seemed we wouldn't have his attention for long. REAP had been hatched several years before by a group of Peace Corps agriculture volunteers working with villagers and the Ministries of Education and Agriculture. It was built on the premise that children who learned the pride, pleasure and profit of having their own gardens while in school would transform into a community of adults who grow their own food and enough to sell to others. It had been successful all over Belize, even here in Double Head Cabbage, but under a different principal. As I was just about to learn.

Tall and lanky, balding slightly, Mr. Fanning suddenly perked up at my question. "The REAP program belonged to the last principal, not to me."

Minutes later we were in his office, and Mr. Fanning was pulling out the bottom drawer of his ancient mahogany desk.

A cascade of seed packets spilled onto the floor, all of them stamped "A Gift from the United States of America." He did this with such flourish I couldn't help feeling like he was making fun of me and the source of the gift.

"No one's interested in gardening here, Mrs. Runkel. It's just too much trouble. I doubt we'll have much use for any of these seeds. Besides, we need Mary, the volunteer, to fill in as a reading teacher. That's how we'll be using her," he said, with a hint of pride, I thought.

"I can really understand it, Mr. Fanning," Dorothy piped in. "With so little water, I know gardening is really hard. And so many of our Belizean families just don't seem to want to garden unless they have a volunteer coaching them. Mary seems to be doing a good job with the reading," she said. "Which days is she here?" she asked Mr. Fanning.

I was looking out the window at the children dressed all in maroon and white in the school yard and wondering why I seemed to be the only one in the room who cared where they got healthy food. "Where is our volunteer?" I asked.

"I'm sure she'll be around the next time we come out," Dorothy said quickly.

Mr. Fanning was preparing to leave. Dorothy thanked him for his time, which had been approximately eight minutes.

"I hope you'll give some thought to gardens next spring," I said. "I hear the government's bringing water to this village, so it will be a lot simpler and could mean healthier and smarter students for you."

"Nice to meet you, Mrs. Lumpel," he said.

My trips out with the other associate directors were far more satisfying. Every possible detail for each visit was written down, I had meetings with volunteers, government officials, teachers and village *alcaldes* (leaders). Inspiring as the work they were doing was, I couldn't help sensing that an injection of new thinking was sorely needed. This was what I was sent here to do and I was eager to do it.

Over the next few weeks, I put together a management plan that revolved around participatory staff meetings, new program designs, stronger volunteer support systems and accountability from each of us to one another, as well as to our Belizean partners. I called on everyone to think of creative solutions for problems that had plagued the post for years.

Everyone responded enthusiastically—except for our Peace Corps employee of nearly thirty years, Dorothy. I stopped by her office one day to find out why she hadn't come to our first staff meeting. I noticed she had one of the nicest offices in this old colonial mansion by the sea. She was finishing up a meeting with some people to whom she didn't introduce me.

"Dorothy," I said, "Don't want to interrupt. Was just wanting to talk about the staff meeting."

"I'm afraid those meetings are just out of the question for me," she said, self-consciously picking up papers from the meeting that had concluded. "I'm just overwhelmed with meetings these days."

"Really? Is something pressing?" I asked. "I thought we'd had consensus that this was a date and time that would work for everyone on the senior staff."

She looked out the window, put both hands on her desk and said in a most officious tone, "The last three Peace Corps directors have had no difficulty with the fact that I'm on the Board of Directors of the YWCA and therefore must attend *all* their meetings. Since they're one of the most important partners the Peace Corps has, I don't see how I could miss, do you?"

"Dorothy, I know the YWCA has been invaluable to us, but your presence here is also. Any chance for a change in timing? You could use the new director as an excuse, I wouldn't mind."

"The only way we could change the time is to violate the agreement Peace Corps directors have had in the past about me and YWCA Board business," she responded in such a patronizing way that I had a flash of anger. Who, after all, was in charge?

At the next staff meeting—minus Dorothy again—we covered plans for the upcoming Thanksgiving workshop for volunteers who'd been in the field for three months and problem areas in each part of the country. Then I asked to be filled in about the history of the REAP program.

"I was a REAP volunteer in Yo Creek," George said. "It was in the early days of the program, and it caught on so well there's now an agricultural junior college up near where I worked. And, the village has its own Farmers' Market that's nearly put the Mexican peddlers out of business."

"Yeah, man. The *George LeBard School of Agriculture*," Francisco teased.

"But seriously, Deedie, it really is the best development tool we have for the rural areas of the country," Austin added. We'll take you out to see some good gardens when you come back."

"It's the type of Belizean-based development Peace Corps wants, and the Education Ministry and the Agriculture Ministry both support it wholeheartedly," George said. "The problem is, Dorothy doesn't much like it. Never has." I was glad to have the real story.

My month-long orientation nearly over, I was rushing to get myself packed for a return to Washington for Christmas, after which I'd be back to begin the assignment that would ultimately last three-and-a-half years. Dorothy had called early that morning to say she'd be taking me to the airport.

"How great," I said.

"I didn't want you thinking I wasn't your friend," she said warmly. "Besides, then I'll be able to take the leftovers from that lovely party you had for us last night, to the orphanage near the YWCA."

She stood at the door to my bedroom watching me fly around throwing things in the duffel. I was sopping wet with perspiration and self-consciousness. I would have been happier taking a cab.

"Whatever are all these little boxes for?" she asked, picking one up off the dresser.

"Oh, it's just a collection I've had for years. I keep my jewelry in them and they remind me of the important people in my life." David had been incredulous that I was making room for them in my bags. I told him they were touchstones to remind me where I'd been and who I was, and they also happened to be good places for jewelry.

"They're awfully pretty," Dorothy said. "Maybe someday you'll tell me more about each one."

"Oh, of course, I will. And I haven't thanked you yet, Dorothy, for coming to the Belize Choral Society concert the other night. I saw you in the audience."

"Well we were certainly impressed that you learned the music so fast and seemed to know *all* the verses of the National Anthem," she said.

∽

Dorothy's relationship with Peace Corps over the next year remained secondary to her involvement in at least a dozen different enterprises around town. She was rarely at meetings and often just "somewhere else." It wasn't unusual for her to enlist other staff members to help on non-Peace Corps projects. Eugene, the driver, or Katherine, the program assistant, often worked on her personal assignments—until I called them both in and told them to stop.

In the meantime, for the first time ever, the entire staff had participated in the development of our program plan and budget for the upcoming year. We'd had a retreat—also the first ever—and flushed out issues that had been simmering beneath the surface for a long time. Out of these, we formed agreements as a staff for how we wanted to interact. *Everyone should pull their own weight* was high on the list.

I finally got to meet Mary, the volunteer from Double Head Cabbage, when she took advantage of my open-door policy one day later in January. She'd grown up on a farm in Iowa, was the daughter of Peace Corps volunteers who'd served in Africa, and was thoroughly frustrated.

"I got all the families in the village together and they *wanted* to plant a garden and Mr. Fanning won't give us the seeds. He says they're his. And Dorothy says she can't make him give them up, and she won't even come out there. Really, Deedie, you should see how the villagers got all the ground prepared. They're even composting. And I don't even know how to teach reading and that's all Mr. Fanning will talk about me doing and I'm sorry for crying but I can't help it." She put her head down in her hands and sobbed.

"We're going to work this out, Mary. I know Mr. Fanning's difficult, but we'll figure out a good strategy. I'll talk to Dorothy. Thank you so much for all you're doing."

Shortly after that, a cable arrived saying Peace Corps/Belize would get all the funds it had requested but had to reduce the staff by one, since we were going to have fewer volunteers (which we'd recommended in our plan).

I knew immediately which staff person it would be but worried that if I fired a community icon, there could be repercussions. I consulted Belize labor laws, the Ambassador and the Peace Corps administrative code. The Ambassador agreed with my assessment of what the situation was and said he appreciated my giving him a heads up.

"One thing I learned early about you, Miss Deedie, is that when you make your mind up, it's made up," he said as I left his office. Thank heaven he didn't know how many butterflies were fluttering in my stomach.

Back in my office, I thought hard about the agreements the staff and I had worked so hard to hammer out and how it must feel to them to know the person with the best office, highest salary and the longest tenure wasn't pulling her weight.

I checked with Dorothy to make sure she planned to keep our bi-weekly meeting date, something I did with each staff member to make sure we were staying on top of our "issues."

"The meetings this time are really important because they're all about the budget," I said.

"I'll be there, don't worry. I've been through many, many of these meetings before," she said wearily.

The big lumbering wooden sail boats were coasting back to shore, their soiled and mildewed pink and blue sails full of wind, their bows brimming with sand to be used in construction projects all over the city. They sailed out empty in the morning, skimming the surface and returned in the late afternoon laden with sand, moving in slow motion.

I watched them from my office as I waited for Dorothy. I was nervous. Though she certainly wasn't the first person I'd ever had to fire, I was anxious, worried about how it was going to play out. Surely she realized there hadn't been wind in her Peace Corps sails for a very long time.

"Here I am," she announced, a little breathless from climbing the stairs. "And I brought you a box." She placed a red heart-shaped plastic box on the table. "It's not much, but I thought it would go nicely with that collection of yours."

Dorothy received the news of her "redundancy" with no emotion whatsoever. I asked her if, after all these years, she might be ready to retire anyway.

She said maybe she was.

When I got to the office the next morning, my boss in Washington was on the phone. "How'd it go with your employee?" he asked.

"I think it went well. I don't think she was totally surprised. And everyone in both the American and Belizean communities seems to accept it," I reported.

"Well, I just want you to know how grateful we are to you for pulling everything together down there. You've done a really wonderful job on every front. Even standing down the Ambassador. We're going to nominate you for a meritorious increase," he said.

"Wow. I wasn't expecting this."

"Well, since as a Peace Corps director you're not getting the 25 per cent differential, it's the least we can do," he said, laughing.

I joined in, grateful that the hardships meriting my differential had nothing to do with sweltering days and poisonous snakes and everything to do with Peace Corps fulfilling its noble mission.

CHAPTER THIRTEEN

The Choice

I woke up to the smell of nail polish. Opening one eye I could see Constance applying what Granny would call circus-girl red polish to her fingernails. It was six o'clock in the morning. That red always seemed to me pretty bold for someone so conservative. But now I knew how she kept them looking so perfect. A pre-dawn touch-up. I scrambled out of bed to get to the pool, leaving Constance to her vapors. We were at a week-long conference on women, and the gulf between our morning activities was yet another indicator of how different we were.

To me, Constance was the living representation of all the things that had eluded me in life. She had degrees from fancy colleges, a successful and secure career, financial independence, could speak another language and knew how to expertly navigate muddy political and diplomatic waters. The longer I was around her, the more I perceived her as being perfect. Her porcelain skin was clear and always evenly powdered. Her clothes were dark, expensive, and correct, and her office had perfect flowers and neat piles at all times. The younger staff at Development Goals International (DGI) would come to me in awe of her vast knowledge and ability to hone in precisely on programs and proposals. This only made me feel more and more inadequate, because I was certain these were not things they would ever say about *me*. All of my deficits were Constance's assets. My psychiatrist tried to get me to see that these comparisons were not only unhealthy, they were also unfounded, but I couldn't hear him. I woke up each morning wishing I could think of something I *was* instead of all the things I wasn't.

Swimming was my hedge against depression. Still is. It makes me feel as if I've accomplished something before the day has really begun. At the end of the day, if everything else has conspired to make me feel hopeless and helpless, I can look back on that swim and know I did at least one thing right. For my long-term health. For each of the people to whom I dedicate a lap. For each of my deepest hopes to which I dedicate a lap—serenity, peace, love.

But swimming wasn't cutting it at that time in my life. I was depressed. Really depressed. And I had been ever since starting my job at the DGI, where Constance was the vice-president. All I wanted to do was swim more, cry or sleep. Crying was winning out, and I was spending increasingly more time in the Ladies Room at work doing just that. To escape the notice of my colleagues, I'd go down to the restroom on the next floor. I wasn't about to acknowledge to anyone on my floor that I was anything other than the Director of Program Development for DGI. Admitting to depression would only make me more depressed.

My return from Belize, where I'd flourished as the Peace Corps director, had not been easy. I was 50-something and finding a new job had been a challenge, especially one that used my leadership skills, was international, interesting, and paid me enough to get us through our college tuition-paying years. I mightily wished I could stay with Peace Corps for the rest of my life, but JFK himself had imposed a five-year rule for staff, making Peace Corps the only federal agency with term limits. As it was, I'd stretched the five years to eight and a half. I had been sought out to be the candidate for head of two Quaker schools, gotten down to the finals and not been chosen (which shouldn't have been a surprise because I have no education credentials). Most of the international jobs I tried for required a second language.

The inescapable conclusion—to me—was that I was useless. I envied my friends who had actual professions, like being a nurse or a professor. On my worst days, I imagined my memorial service, or a scenario in which my car could leave the road and not hurt anyone but me. My passport picture issued at the time shows a hollow-eyed old woman who, with antlers, could pass for a deer in headlights.

When DGI's president, Jim Myers, hired me for a position that had never before existed in the firm, he told me outright he was taking a chance on me. Especially since I was definitely not the person Constance would have chosen for this job. Jim had spent much of his career working in Latin America, which definitely had an impact on his management style. I told my friends he'd been around too many macho dictators.

At the time, that kind of comment from Jim rolled off my back. I was simply thrilled to be in management rather than public relations or communications, positions I'd filled so often I could do it in my sleep. The job also gave me the chance to continue working with young professionals, as I had in Belize. Most exciting of all, DGI's work, as an international consulting firm building community-based programs in the developing world, was right in my area of interest. And nearly all its funding came from the United States Agency for International Development (USAID) and large foundations, players I felt comfortable working with.

But despite what had seemed to me to be a good match for my career, I'd slipped into that downhill slide. Jim and Constance knew what they were doing; I became convinced I didn't. My initial resistance to getting psychiatric help was tied up in my belief that if I could just get better at doing the job, my bosses would start acknowledging my abilities and conditions at work would improve. But when I started feeling suicidal, I gave in and started taking an antidepressant. I tried to imagine what my life would be like if I believed I was valuable and no less worthwhile than Constance. Was this what Zoloft could accomplish? I strongly doubted it. My psychiatrist was full of questions, including, "Might the situation at work with Jim and Constance have thrown you back to your childhood, with Jim as your father and Constance your mother?" Where does that get me, I wondered. So what if it has?

"How's work coming on the Guatemala proposal? Isn't it due next week?" It was Jim, phoning the office from his vacation spot in Maine.

"Don't you remember, Jim, we decided to pass on it? We all determined we don't have the capacity. Remember?" I spoke confidently. One thing I'd learned was to talk strong if I was talking to Jim. Otherwise, he might get mad.

He got mad anyway.

"I don't give a rat's ass about any of yours and Constance's *processes*. We're going for this and we'll get it. I know the director of USAID in Guatemala, and we'll get Arnie to move up there from Costa Rica and run it. What is the matter with you that you don't get it?" he shouted. "You'd better get to work, Runkel, right now. Do you hear me? We're going for it and we're going to get it."

"But, Jim. I don't see how we can do it now in such a short time," I protested.

"Get to work, Deedie. Now. No more excuses."

Deflated and depleted, I hung up the phone and went into Constance's office to relate my conversation with Jim. Any sympathy or empathy she might have had for my position was usurped by her typical determination to "carry on."

"It really is outrageous at this point to press for this," I blurted out.

"Outrage isn't going to get this proposal in, Deedie. Let's figure out what all needs to be done," she said, leafing through the voluminous document that described everything that had to be presented in the proposal. "I'm going on vacation tomorrow, so you're going to be quite busy; I can only give you a smidgen of time," she said, smiling.

I never knew quite how to receive Constance's smile. Was she just being the consummate professional? Submitting proposals to USAID was an art, one practiced by many firms in the Washington area, most of them much larger than ours. Successful bidders were generally those who already had a presence in the host country, had local partner organizations, and had people on staff or in their stable of experts who were known for doing successful projects. DGI had none of the above in Guatemala and little experience with the types of programs the proposal was asking for.

With both Constance and Jim gone, how to begin? I broadcast an email to everyone they and I knew, even remotely, inside and outside the building: "Send me your ideas and dreams for this former war zone in Guatemala, now known as the Peace Zone."

Sani, the switchboard operator, turned out to be our savior. She arrived breathlessly in my office with a flyer that had literally just fallen out of the fax machine. It was from Rigoberta Menchù's organization, looking for partners in Washington, DC. Rigoberta! This Guatemalan indigenous activist was one of my heroes. I couldn't believe it. She'd just won the Nobel Peace prize for her work in the Peace Zone, aiding indigenous people, who'd been targeted by the government for years. I called immediately. After a short conversation, I asked Eduardo, her representative, what kind of help they were looking for. He said they needed someone to sponsor Rigoberta's first trip to Washington.

"Eduardo," I said, barely able to contain my excitement, "We can do that for you. We can set up visits to members of Congress and at the State Department and the World Bank. We would be happy to host a reception for her."

"This is very good, Deedie," he said, "But how could we possibly repay you for your work?"

"Well, Eduardo . . . . ," I began slowly, formulating my pitch. By the end of the day, we had signed on as the partner for our proposal the most important woman in Guatemala. And a Nobel Laureate at that.

Constance had asked that we be sure to put a copy of the final proposal on her desk so she could read it upon her return, which I actually looked forward to. I'd ended up being delighted with the results. The young talented and brilliant staff had pulled together with me to make it a very compelling and competitive document. Maybe this job *was* something I could do. During my daily swim, I tried to follow the doctor's advice and focus on what I was doing well, rather than what I wasn't doing well.

"Well, Deedie, this isn't exactly what I would have done with this proposal, but Jim says we're going to get it in any event," Constance said after leafing through our opus. Her bright red fingernails tapped her leather Daytimer. "Let's do lunch today and catch up on what else has been going on around here."

"Isn't it great that we get to meet Rigoberta? She's going to be the key to our success, *if* we get it," I said. "Can you believe that it was *Sani* who saw the potential?"

"Oh, we'll get it, rest assured of that," she said. "Jim's contacts are ironclad. And Sani was just doing her job, picking up the fax, bringing it to you," she said.

My spirits plummeted once more. I left her office and took the elevator to the next floor down, went straight to the Ladies Room and sat in a stall and sobbed. Why couldn't Constance give me at least a little bit of encouragement? Someone from another office heard me and asked if I was okay. I mustered a muffled, "Yes, thanks," and hoped she wouldn't recognize me.

※

With Christmas around the corner, word came that we'd won the contract. It was something close to seven million dollars. Everyone was excited and delighted but me. Suddenly I couldn't imagine how we were going to do all we said we would in the proposal. I felt totally responsible *and* totally at a loss as to how to proceed. The next step would be the development of an action plan, a process that often takes a long time and much negotiating with USAID and other partners in the host country. How could I work with Guatemalans if I didn't speak Spanish? The final contract would hang in the balance until the action plan was accepted.

Much as I love Christmastime, I dreaded its arrival that year. Never being sure of where I stood with Jim and Constance had scraped my self-esteem bare. My spirits were sagging so badly that I begged off my usual job of organizing the DGI holiday party. All I wanted was some measure of peace for myself. The young staff with whom I worked had become my only bulwark against what I increasingly perceived as "enemy"—Constance and Jim. I'd wake up each morning dreading whatever indignity might be in my path that day, but then I'd remember Alain and Abby, Christian and Sani, and lifted by their respect, I'd pull myself out of bed.

The day after Constance left to spend her Christmas in Europe, I arrived at work to find an elegantly wrapped gift from her on my desk. Gold paper with dark green grosgrain ribbon. Nervously, I unwrapped the package and lifted out a miniature oblong Russian lacquered box. On the lid is painted a figure that might be Father Christmas moving along the cobbled street, though the sword in his hand could convince you otherwise. A small skyline of roofs appears in the distance, a bright red rooster crowing from his perch at the peak.

Her note indicated it was for my collection. How ever on earth did she know about that? I couldn't remember telling her. I certainly knew she'd never seen the bureau in my bedroom. Did Constance know me better than I thought she did? In her perfect, small handwriting, she wrote something about how much she had enjoyed working with me this year, especially on the Guatemala proposal, and how great it was that we'd won the contract. Did she really mean this, or was she just saying what a vice president should say to a staff member? I'd lost my ability to hear or accept anything positive about myself.

Just after the holidays, Jim announced to me I was being sent to Guatemala to develop and write the action plan. When Constance found out, she arrived in my office to tell me what she thought was needed in a good action plan, and how it was going to be a tough assignment for me since I didn't speak Spanish, and by the way, Jim's friend Arnie (with whom I'd be working) was not the easiest person to be around. "Bonne chance," she said, shaking her head and giving me one of her half smiles.

I panicked, but Jim would hear none of it. Who else should go except the proposal's primary author, he wanted to know. "Just go down there and do it." When I reminded him I didn't speak Spanish, he reminded me I had Arnie.

"Jim," I said, tears welling up, "I'm depressed. I don't think I can handle it."

He looked at me squarely and said it would do me good to be away for as long as it took to get the job done. "Stay away for a month or six weeks if you have to," he said.

My head and heart unraveled further during the five weeks of work in Guatemala. I became increasingly certain that the reason Jim sent me down there was to get me out of the office, to give me something to do preliminary to getting rid of me permanently. Arnie was a pro, no reason why he couldn't do the action plan alone. I felt superfluous. What had begun as an illusion fueled by anxiety and depression took root in my mind as fact. When I returned to DC, I'd be fired from my job, I just knew it.

That eventuality became uppermost in my mind. I couldn't let go of it. It became my constant companion. Each evening I spent some time role-playing the final encounter with Jim. I thought of calling the psychiatrist to see what he thought, but I couldn't bring myself to make an international call on the subject. Besides, I couldn't face more of his Constance-and-Jim-as-mother-father theory.

Whenever I talked to David back in Washington, I'd prepare him for "the inevitable."

"If you do get fired, we'll deal with it. Just don't worry, sweetie," David would say. "We're going on vacation as soon as you're done and you can put it all behind you."

Under this shadow, I'd start each day with a swim, then a full day of research, writing and meetings at the USAID/Guatemala office, then head back to the hotel room for some tears and an attempt at sleep. My appetite was non-existent.

Room service brought me jug after jug of limeade, which had become my staff of life.

At last everything was ready, and the final presentation to USAID bigwigs was scheduled. The last thing I needed was approval of the action plan by Jim and Constance, but I couldn't get them on the phone. They were always busy or out of the office when I called. I was frantic. In desperation, I'd faxed more than twenty-five pages to them the night before the presentation.

The next morning was dark and wintry. The only light at the pool was an eerie reflection from the dining room above. Instead of peace, each lap brought forth a new anxiety. I rushed back to the room to call David. My voice was flat, hushed.

"Jim and Constance haven't approved my presentation, and it's in just a few hours. I don't know how we're going to pay for Sara's tuition or anything else . . . ,"

"Just get through it, Deedie. You're almost done. You'll do fine today. Steve White called from Seattle last night and said to send you his love. Soon you'll be back here with me and the kids. Just try not to worry anymore. I love you," he said before hanging up.

I dialed the DGI office. While the international connection was clicking through, I practiced to see if I could make my voice sound confident. "Constance! Jim!" I said out loud, cheerily as I could. Jim's secretary, Pam, came on the line.

"Hold on, Deedie. They've been going over all the paper that came through the fax last night."

First, Jim. "What *possessed* you to send a massive fax like this? Jesus, woman, what have you been doing down there?"

"Jim, we don't have much time. I need to have your feedback now. I need to know if the budget's okay. I need to know if I can present this today. I'm supposed to be on the evening flight out of here." My voice was plaintive, roiled with uncertainty.

"Constance, what do you think of this package she's broken the bank to send us?

Were we told anything about this supposed official presentation today, or the fact that our woman in Guatemala is trying to get out of there this afternoon?"

"Jim, Jim," I cut in. "That's why I've been trying to get a hold of you guys, to tell you about USAID wanting me to make the presentation. I wasn't trying to conceal anything."

"Deedie, this is Constance. Of course we knew about the presentation. The director from down there called about it last week. We just wanted to know *what* you were going to present. And I'm afraid I still can't tell from all this paper. It's certainly not the way *I* would have done it, but it's a plan, and that's what they want."

I was so nervous my voice cracked every time I opened my mouth. I was stuttering. My mouth was dry. My hands were starting to shake again. Jim kept trying to get in. I was sure it was to fire me.

"I'm confident you'll paint a good picture during your presentation," Constance continued. "And watch out with that budget. They're going to ding you for having so much travel between Washington and Guatemala. To sum up, Jim, it isn't the way I would have done it, but we don't have much choice at this point."

"So go show the flag, Runkel," Jim said. "Are you okay?"

"I'm okay. I've got to rush now to get there. Wish me luck!"

Less than three hours later, I was chatting with the USAID/ Guatemala staff, the presentation over. Nearly thirty had turned out to hear what we planned to do, how and when.

To my amazement, it had all made perfect sense as I was saying it, and I gained strength as I went along. I told little anecdotes. I revealed more about myself—a Quaker proud to be working in an area the American Friends Service Committee had targeted. Even as I said it, I worried Constance would have found it "unprofessional." At the end, everyone clapped and clapped. Some even stood. Arnie told me later he would call it a standing ovation!

❧

After a break for our family vacation, I returned to DGI filled with dread. Jim called me in. *Here it comes,* I thought. My mind went to how I could die driving on Dale Drive, not far from the psychiatrist's office. Constance and Jim were both present. An ominous sign. They must have talked about this. Jim spoke first.

"We think you are the ideal person to be our first official Director of Communications, Deedie. Doesn't that sound like a perfect thing? With your writing and schmoozing skills, you could do it with one hand tied behind your back. You could really put us on the map. What do you think?" Jim asked.

"Wouldn't that be something totally in your comfort zone?" Constance added.

Jim was up, moving around the room. He sat down in the chair next to me and leaned over close.

"This is the perfect job for you at the perfect time, don't you think? Constance agrees it would be best. You know the press. You know Capitol Hill. You've got contacts all over DC. You know how to do everything to get DGI to where we want to be. You're the key to our achieving our vision." He put his hands on my knees for a fleeting second and then was up and around again, turning back to see how I was reacting.

I swallowed hard. They were patronizing me. I'd done that kind of communications work so many times before in my career that Communications felt to me like a "fluff" job. Director of Program Development had been a job with real gravitas, drawing on management and leadership skills. Tears were coming to my eyes even though I willed them not to. No matter how I looked at Jim's offer, I saw it as a huge demotion.

"I'll think about it. Thanks for your confidence. This is my night to volunteer at the soup kitchen. Right now," I managed to say as I escaped, nearly tripping over Constance, whose red-tipped fingers were clasped together tightly in her lap.

"Jim's right, Deedie. We really need someone to take charge of our communications work," she called after me. "It's your strength. You think hard about it." Her voice sounded so ingratiating that my commitment to nonviolence was sorely tested.

Years later, Jim and I talked about this moment at DGI. He was shocked to think I'd understood it as a demotion.

"We would never have said such a thing or made such an offer if we thought it would hurt you." He gave me one of his direct blue-eyed looks, but this one filled with unexpected kindness. "I knew you were already hurting," he said.

A few days after the communications job offer, I woke up unable to speak. My voice was gone. I didn't have a cold. I didn't have a cough. I just couldn't talk. David called DGI to say I couldn't come in. When the phone began ringing, I didn't know if I should pick up. I could only make rasping sounds. On the tenth ring, I answered.

"Deedie, it's Abby. I want to come over to see you. You don't have to talk. I'll do the talking, okay?"

"Uh-huh," I whispered.

We sat at the dining room table with tea. Abby had been through her own rough patch at DGI recently, but had somehow put herself on what seemed like a positive, perfect course. I was jealous. If only I could have been that smart when I was young . . .

"Deedie, I don't want you to be so unhappy. No wonder your voice has gone away. Your whole spirit has disappeared. You need to get back to a place where you feel like you belong. Figure out what's right *for you*."

Every time I tried to say something, all I did was croak. Tears streamed down my face. Abby was trying to be helpful. She believed in me. But somehow, I was feeling demoted by her as well. What was the matter with me that a junior staff member was compelled to come to the rescue? Why was everything so hard? I could hardly bear it.

❧

Two days later, I returned to work. My voice was slightly more reliable, though I could never predict when it was going to give out. Being on the phone was tough.

When I got home that night, I was surprised to find our friend Steve there from Seattle.

"What the hell are you doing here?" I croaked with delight. Seeing a favorite Peace Corps colleague was practically enough to make me feel human again.

"Deed, I thought you could use a friend," Steve said. He'd known it was an emergency when he talked to David. "David told me you couldn't come to the phone because you didn't have a *voice*. So I said to myself, *If Deedie's run out of a voice, she's in bad shape*."

The next thing I knew he was asking me directly if I was thinking about harming myself. I admitted I had picked out a spot where I wouldn't hurt anyone else. Steve had always asked me the hard questions, always inspired the truth in me. I could never get over how good he was at it.

At first I was embarrassed that I'd caused such concern that he would fly across the country to take care of me. But soon I settled into the warmth and affirmation of friendship. As I fell asleep that night, I believed two things I hadn't when the day started. One, I hadn't really been fired. And two, my life was important enough that a friend had traveled a very long distance to convince me of its value. And maybe, maybe, *maybe* that's exactly what everyone—David, Jim, Constance, Abby and the doctor were trying to get me to hear.

Steve stayed for two days. His presence and support helped me reach a new place. I was a highly-skilled, highly-functioning professional with many skills, skills that could be used in many different ways in many different settings. It was up to *me* to decide what and where that would be. And it wasn't DGI.

I went into my office, packed and left. In my mind, I could hear Constance saying, *"It's not the way I would have done it."* But it's the way I did it—my choice, my way—and for me that was finally the right way.

CHAPTER FOURTEEN

Toward the Light

An image of my first grandchild filled the computer screen. I was sitting in the lobby at the Comfort Inn in Hiroshima, Japan. Unable to contain myself, I let out a screech and then began to sob uncontrollably. Ramona Meriwether Runkel. Not even an hour old.

This was my second visit to Hiroshima, this time as a member of the Rogue Valley Peace Choir from Oregon. We were the first American group invited to be part of the city's formal observance of Hiroshima Day, the sixth of August, commemorating that infamous day in 1945 when the first nuclear bomb ever used was dropped on Japan by the United States. I'd signed on for this peace journey before I had the slightest inkling that it would coincide with Ramona's birth.

It was five o'clock in the morning and I had come down to the lobby to check my email. I've always loved being up before anyone else. It gives me a part of the day just to myself. I had another reason this morning. The night before David had sent a disturbing email. Mel, Marshall's wife, had a headache she couldn't shake. Her due date was at hand, and the headache could signal pre-eclampsia. I hadn't slept all night and at the very first light of day, I'd gotten up to see if there was any news. Instead there she was! Ramona.

I stared into the screen, still weeping, looking for genetic signs she belonged to me. Tears spilled down my cheeks, flooding the tiny napkin I was dabbing at my face with. I recognized Marshall's huge hand encasing her tiny bottom. *Was her face the shape of Mel's? Her forehead isn't high like a Beeson's. Those lips might be Runkel. She's not quite as bald as Lucy was.*

"Are you going to be all right, madam?" Startled, I looked up to see I was surrounded by the hotel staff. The head clerk was bending over toward my damp face.

"This is my *granddaughter*," I exclaimed. "She was just born. In Portland, Oregon. This is my *first* grandchild. I am so happy to be here in Hiroshima, but I am very excited about what has happened in my family." I was trying to regain my composure.

The English-speaking head clerk began translating what I'd said for his colleagues. Suddenly they all thrust their hands together and began bowing toward me.

"Obaa-chan, Obaa-chan," they smiled, bowing furiously, greeting me as the honored grandmother. One of them ran over to the desk and returned with a rose in a vase.

"Obaa-chan. Good," she said, bowing and presenting it to me with both hands.

I wanted to hug them but knew it would be culturally more appropriate if I just stood up and bowed back.

"Me," I pointed to myself, towering over my fellow celebrants. "Obaa-chan. Very, very happy. Very good. Thank you so much." All of a sudden I was jumping up and down between bows. I had never felt so much energy flowing through me all at once.

Laughing happily among themselves, the staff returned to their posts behind the desk and in the breakfast room. I sat back down again and peered at the computer screen. Another picture. Ramona on her mother's chest. Two very happy, albeit sleepy-looking girls. Beautiful. And a note saying the labor had been amazingly swift and all was well.

I wrote back: "Ramona's birth has already brought much joy to Hiroshima, my dears. It may be Ramona Day there, but it is Hiroshima Day here, and I plan now to go to the Peace Park. I am so happy I may create an international incident of some sort."

A new me left the hotel that morning and set out along the streets of the city. I was a grandmother. A new generation of our family was now present. What would this mean for me, for Ramona, for all of us? Would I someday be crossing this busy boulevard holding hands with her? Showing her through the Peace Museum, introducing her to this ancient culture? Would I show her the hotel lobby where she was "born" for me? Maybe she would love to sing as much as I do. Maybe here she would she call me Obaa-chan. Would she be as passionate as I have been for so many years about creating a more peaceful world?

As I approached the Peace Plaza, I could see the famous Genbaku Dome off in the distance, a hollow shell of a building, the only one still standing here at Ground Zero.

A young boy scout handed me a bouquet of blue and yellow flowers.

"For sale?" I asked, reaching for my wallet.

"For the memorial," he said, matter-of-factly, turning to point to the beautiful display just ahead at the edge of the plaza. Overnight, structures had gone up that now ringed the plaza.

Risers were banked with multitudes of flowers and candles. Signs above each one identified which group of the deceased was being honored and which group was the sponsor. Later in the day, people would make the circuit around the plaza, pausing at each memorial in respect. "No charge," the scout said.

I reverently placed my bouquet at the first memorial, in my name and Ramona's.

As I approached the acres of concrete plaza surrounding the buildings of the Peace Museum, I noticed a group of people lined up at one side. There must have been about 200 of them in more-or-less even rows about ten deep. They all seemed quite relaxed, many of them in sweat suits, all chatting among themselves. I knew that none of the official events would begin until after 8:15 a.m., the time the bomb fell. What could be happening just before 6 a.m.? What were they assembled for?

I stood a little off to the side, not wanting to be conspicuous but also not wanting to miss an event if there was going to be one. One person in the group saw me and gestured for me to join them. I smiled and bowed, but kept moving slowly around, feeling a little bit shy. Suddenly, without warning, a horn blared from the loud speaker. I looked at my watch—six a.m. sharp. Everyone straightened up, eyes forward. Seconds later music began, interspersed with someone calling out something to the group, and they all began moving in unison. Aerobics! I'd come upon an exercise class. Perfect.

I lined up at the end of one row and began concentrating hard in an effort to copy those around me. Just as I'd get one move right, the coach would yell out something and everyone would switch to a new move. I'd struggle to re-calibrate my arms and legs fast enough to keep up. Perspiration poured off me. Later I would ask my Japanese friend Hideko, the Peace Choir member who had initiated our journey, why they did each move only three times in Japan. "Deedie, my dear, she said with a wry smile. "Seven times. They do each move *seven times.*"

I was so focused on what I was doing that at first I didn't notice that several of those around me were laughing so hard they had to stop doing the exercises. Some had turned around and were pointing at me and giggling at something behind me. I finally stopped and looked where they were pointing. Just behind me was a television camera that had been documenting my frantic efforts. One of the crew thrust a microphone toward my face. Without missing a beat, and with a big smile, I said into the camera, "Me, Obaa-chan, today! Yay!" and did a little jumping jack. My fellow exercisers all clapped and began chanting, "Obaa-chan, Obaa-chan!" over the din of the loudspeaker. The television crew, which turned out to be from Germany, finished their segment and packed up. Everyone went back to exercising. Only now can I look back and imagine the scene they'd captured—a tall, grey-haired Western lady flailing about among dozens of Japanese half her height. Without even planning it, I'd created an international incident on Ramona's birthday. I couldn't have been more delighted.

Our Peace Choir's first official event of the day was at the school from which Hideko had graduated. Located within Ground Zero, their annual Hiroshima Day commemoration is held in memory of the faculty and students whose lives were lost to the atom bomb. Our Hideko was the keynote speaker this year. Eleven years old the day of the bombing, she recounted her experiences to the student body: how she'd spent the rest of that day searching fruitlessly for her mother, how she'd gone to the river, remembering her mother's instructions to always look for water. We all ached for Hideko as if her pain was fresh, not over sixty years old. Even though she spoke in Japanese, the language of her suffering was, for us spellbound choir members, universal.

As I looked at the faces of each student currently attending the school, I wondered how they would absorb Hideko's story into their everyday lives, filled as they must be with academics, sports, text messaging and friends? Part of me wanted Ramona to never know about Hideko's searing pain, while another part fervently hoped that the pain in Ramona's own life would always be buffered by the love of family and friends. At the end of the ceremony, we lined up to place a flower on the school's memorial. I placed mine and lingered fleetingly, praying for Ramona's safe passage through life in a world filled with contradictions . . . . and, I knew, love.

A few months later, Ramona had her first Christmas. She and I were home alone in Ashland and I was carrying her in my arms. The rest of the family was out doing last-minute shopping. Once again, I was filled with the hopes and dreams and visions that had materialized the day of her birth. As we walked through the house, I introduced her to the family she had been born into.

Here's Granny's dining room table, Ramona. That would be your great-great grandmother. This is the table where you'll sit for many Christmases and Thanksgivings and breakfasts, just like Granny, then Mimi, then me, your Cookie, and then your own daddy when he was growing up. Granny was a demon about manners, just like I am.

A picture of my parents. Here are your great-grandparents, Mimi and Poppy. How they would love to know you are here, how important it would be to them that your dad is so thrilled to have you.

This is a painting done for your great Uncle Bill by his friend, Dan Piel. Uncle Bill was quite an inspiration, Ramona. I'm sorry you'll never know him in person. He would love you very much and tell you stories (and read you stories) and write stories about you.

This beautiful box with the bird's eggs in it. That is something your Auntie Netts created. Isn't it wonderful? Auntie Netts can do anything she sets her mind to.

I was just warming up, headed for pictures of Lucy and Sara when Ramona started fussing.

"Let's play some music," I said to her, shifting her to my hip so I could manage to put in a disk. Seconds later, we were swaying back and forth as the first chords of "The Messiah" came on.

"Listen, Ramona," I said. "In just a few minutes the singing will begin, and we can sing 'The Hallelujah Chorus' together." We swayed and sang, Ramona joining for the first time one of her family's favorite holiday traditions.

"Stay, Cookie. And I want Big Poppa to stay here." Ramona was begging us not to leave. We were in Portland for the weekend to see Marsh and Mel and get another squeeze from our favorite girl, now all of three years old.

"Cookie and Poppa have to go back to Ashland," I said. "But here's something to keep in a special place until we're here again." I held out the small object.

Ramona ran over to see what it was, her brown silky hair swinging in her face. I put the tiny box in her hand and watched her fingers quickly close around it.

"Let's put it up here on the bookshelf," I suggested, carefully opening her hand. "It will help you remember what you did with Cookie, and how you felt."

It's no bigger than a quarter, this varnished brown box with a blue baby bird perched on top. Small and perfect like her. Bright with varnish, like her big brown eyes are with intelligence. The baby blue bird on the lid looks safe and secure as she is, but perched in such a way that it can fly off when it's ready.

I had a different box to give her at first, one made in Japan, tiny and white with gold-tipped legs and pale pink roses on the sides and top. It had come from David's mom's dresser to mine just a few years before. I was thrilled to have a memento of someone whose influence on my life has been so significant. Nana is the mother I always wanted. One day when I was dusting my dresser, that delicate little box fell off and broke into too many pieces to mend. I was upset at first that this keepsake of the past wouldn't get passed on to Ramona as planned. But I'd learned something during my journey to the land where that box had been made. Long after the pieces are cleared away, loving memories continue to mend whatever has been broken.

It's hard to escape our past, for it is always present. Sifting through all our boxes, we find what makes us authentic, to ourselves and to others. We see the shape of our past and the long shadow it casts on our future. And we see that as each lid is lifted, more light shines in.

I continue to turn toward that light, for myself . . . . and for Ramona.

Acknowledgments

This book has its roots in relationships.

When I left Penn State in the winter of 1963 my academic advisor, author John Barth, elicited from me the promise that I would never stop writing. I've only more or less kept that promise. Motherhood, a career, community have all encroached on my writing life.

Forty years later, on another side of the continent, I was ready to write. I joined a writing group led by Shoshana Alexander, also an author. Every two weeks for the last six years, I've brought the group drafts and re-drafts of the chapters herein. Under Shoshana's brilliant tutelage, I finally recognized my own voice and nurtured its growth. My fellow writers Susan Dumond, Carol Hwochinsky and Carolyn Shaffer have actively and lovingly helped propel me and this book forward.

Luckily, the book and I have been in the hands of a gifted teacher, which is what Shoshana Alexander is, first and foremost. As both teacher and editor, she has taught me to mine the landscapes of my life to give them a literary impact and universality unapparent to me at the outset. Her keen intellect and endless encouragement have been integral, essential ingredients to this process.

Kim Meek's design and Judy Pavlik's photography enhance these pages in ways that words could not.

The eyes and minds of readers Bob Edwards, Susan Kanaan, Lisa Loomer, Lee Neff, Barbara Rosen and Tanya Russ brought new wisdom and weight to the book.

Many boxes remain on the dresser, their lids not yet lifted. Those who gave them are nonetheless important parts of the collection that is my life: Abigail Calkins Aguirre, Avery Beeson, Virginia Beeson, Kate Boucher, Susie Crowley, Susan Dumond, Dorothy Iams, Laurissa, Anne Gray Liversidge, Ellen Bleecker Liversidge, Sarah Lenzi, Marina, Manuela Reyes, Mara Shall, Svetlana, Nicole Vanasse and Yelena.

My family's forbearance with this project has been monumental and I want them to know how much I appreciate it. The prospect of having their innermost lives shared with the world has been an uneasy one for David, Nettie, Marsh, Lucy and Sara.

David Runkel's ability to withstand the regular onslaught of draft and re-draft over the course of six years has been just plain heroic, and he's done it with loving encouragement, insight and creativity.

If my words are the bricks, these people are surely the mortar of this book.

About the Author

Donnan (Deedie) Runkel draws upon a full-storied life that began in suburban Philadelphia, Pennsylvania, where she grew up, and led to Washington, D.C. where she helped launch the antinuclear organization Peace Links, before joining Peace Corps headquarters staff as Director of Public Affairs. She served as director of Peace Corps/Belize, and later as an international consultant. She is currently president of the Rotary Club of Ashland. She and her husband David Runkel have three grown children and one grandchild (so far). They live in Ashland, Oregon, with Cappy, an aging chocolate lab, where they are the proprietors of Anne Hathaway's Bed & Breakfast and Garden Suites.